GREAT
ANSWERS
to
TOUGH
INTERVIEW
QUESTIONS

GREAT ANSWERS to TOUGH INTERVIEW QUESTIONS

How to Get the Job You Want

Martin John Yate

Kogan
Page

First published in the United States of America
in 1985 by Bob Adams Inc, Boston, Massachusetts

Copyright © Martin John Yate 1985

This edition first published in Great Britain
in 1986 by Kogan Page Ltd, 120 Pentonville Road,
London N1 9JN
Reprinted 1987

British Library Cataloguing in Publication Data

Yate, Martin John
  Great answers to tough interview questions.
  1. Employment interviewing
  I. Title
  650.1′4   HF5549.5.I6

  ISBN 1-85091-238-6

Printed and bound in Great Britain by
Biddles Ltd, Guildford and King's Lynn

Dedication

To my father Bill Yate who showed me that where there is a will, there is a way to reach your goals with consideration and manners.

Acknowledgements

I would like to acknowledge my running mate Jill for her quiet support, my son Peregrine for his noisy distractions, and my dear mother who wonders when I'm coming home to get a real job.

Contents

Introduction

Why another book about interviewing? Because the others stop at that critical point when the tough questions start flying. They lack the practical advice of what to do in the heat of battle. *Great Answers to Tough Interview Questions* first helps you to arrange interviews, then gets right to the heart of your biggest interview dread: 'How on earth do I answer that one?' It takes command where the others admit defeat.

Here you get over seventy of the tough, sneaky, mean and low-down questions that interviewers love to throw at you. I show you what the interviewer is seeking to find out about you with each one, and explain how best to reply. After each explanation you get a sample answer and a unique way to customise the sample to your individual circumstances. The examples themselves come from real life, something that someone like you did on the job that got them noticed and helped them to get ahead in their careers.

Perhaps you are trying to land your first job, or are returning to the workplace, or maybe you're a seasoned executive taking another step up the ladder of success. Whoever you are, this book will help you because every interviewer consistently tries to evaluate every candidate in the same three ways: are you able to do the job, are you willing to put in the effort to make the job a success, and finally, the interviewing manager wants to know if you are manageable.

In interviewing for a new job you will meet two types of interviewer. The first is the 'consciously competent', a professionally trained interviewer who has a carefully structured plan for revealing all your warts and blemishes. The second is the 'unconscious incompetent', who is equally dangerous and bases judgements on gut reactions and nothing more. The book helps you to identify and shine with both of these characters.

The job interview is a measured and ritualistic mating dance in which the best partners whirl away with the glittering prizes. The steps of this dance are the thrust and parry, give-and-take, question-and-response that make meaningful business conversation. Learn the steps and you too can join the dance.

Your partner in the dance is the interviewer, who will lead with tough questions that carry subtleties hidden from the untrained ear. You will learn how to recognise these questions within questions. And with this knowledge, you will be cool, calm, and collected while other candidates are falling apart with attacks of interview nerves.

Just recently a young lady was doing very well on an interview for a high pressure job in a television studio. The interviewer wanted to know how she would react in the sudden stressful situations common in tv and got his answer by asking, 'You know I don't really think you are suitable for the job, wouldn't you be better off in another company?' The job hunter got up with wounded pride and stormed out in a huff. She never knew how close she was to success or how easy it would have been to land that job. The interviewer smiled; he'd caught her out with a tough question. Did the interviewer mean what he said? What was really behind the question? How could she have handled it and got the job? The great answers are awaiting you.

The job interview has many similarities to good social conversation. Job offers always go to the interviewee who can turn a one-sided examination of skills into a dynamic exchange between two professionals. Here you will learn the techniques to excite and hold your interviewer's attention, at the same time promoting yourself as the best candidate for the job.

Great Answers will carry you successfully into and out of the worst interviews you could ever face. It is written in four interconnected parts. Each readies you for the interview and selection process in a distinctive way. 'The Well-Stocked Briefcase' gets you ready for the fray. You will quickly learn to build a curriculum vitae with broad appeal, plus a unique customising technique guaranteed to make your application stand out as something special.

We are a nation anxious to work, yet the cry goes out that there is no work to be had. Some find it easier to cry out against the darkness than dare to light a candle lest a finger get burned. When you know where and how to look you will find the mysterious hidden job market the headhunters talk about. Thousands of jobs at all levels that never reach the newspapers. You will learn how to tap in at the source.

Once you are ready for action 'Getting to Square One' examines all the approaches to getting job interviews and teaches you simple and effective ways to set up multiple interviews. The section ends with techniques to steer you successfully through those increasingly common telephone interviews.

'Great Answers to the Toughest Questions' gives you just that, and teaches you some valuable business lessons that will contribute to your future success. All successful companies look for the same things in their employees, and everything they are looking for you have or can develop. Not possible? I'll prove it to you with the twenty key personality traits which every successful company wants you to show them.

'Finishing Touches' assures that 'out-of-sight-out-of-mind' will not apply to you after leaving the interview. You will even discover how to get a job offer after you have been turned down for the position. Most importantly, the sum of these techniques will give you tremendous self-confidence when you go to an interview: no more jitters, no more sweaty palms.

If you want to know how business works and what know-how business people look for in employees, how to locate, approach and sell yourself at the interview, this book is for you.

Great Answers to Tough Interview Questions delivers what you need to win the job of your dreams. Now get to it, step ahead in your career when you give Great Answers to Tough Interview Questions.

Part 1
The Well-Stocked Briefcase

Out there in the concrete 'forest' of your profession hide many companies. Some major corporations, some small family affairs, and some in between. They all have something in common, and that's *problems*. To solve these problems, companies need people. Anyone who is ever employed for any job is a problem-solver. Think about your present job function: What problems would occur if you weren't there? That's why you were hired, to take care of those problems.

Being a problem-solver is good, but companies prefer to appoint someone who also understands what business is all about. There are three lessons you should remember:

1. Companies are in business to make money. People have loyalty to companies; companies have loyalty only to the bottom line. They make money by being more economical and saving money. They make money by being efficient and saving time. And if they save time, they save money, and have more time to make more money.
2. Companies and you are exactly alike. You both want to make as much money as possible in as short a time as possible. This allows you to do the things you really want with the rest of your time.
3. When the economy is good, you have the whip hand and can dictate the terms. This is called a *seller's market*. When the economy is bad, the employer has the whip hand and can dictate the terms; this is called a *buyer's market*.

Lesson 1 tells you the three things every company is interested in. Lesson 2 recognises that you really have the same goals as the company. Lesson 3 says that anyone with any sense wants to be in a seller's market.

If you look for jobs one at a time, you put yourself in a buyer's market. If you implement my advice you will have multiple interviews because you'll be able to handle the toughest questions, and you'll get multiple job offers. This will give you the whip hand and will put you in a seller's market.

Operating in a seller's market requires knowing who, where, and what your buyers are in the market for, then being ready with the properly packaged product.

In Part 1, you will see how to identify all the companies that could be in need of your services. You will discover names of the chairman, those on the board, those in management; company sales volume; complete lines of company services or products; and size of the operation. You will evaluate and package your professional skills in a method guaranteed to have appeal to every employer. And you will discover highly desirable professional skills that you never thought you had.

A well-stocked briefcase requires more than looking idly through the sits vacant. It means a little discipline, a little effort. But aren't your professional goals worth the effort? It will take a couple of days' work to get geared up.

Your first action should be a trip to the library (taking sufficient paper and pens). Take some sandwiches; there is no feeling in the world like eating lunch on the library steps.

Chapter 1
Discovering What's Out There

At the library, walk in purposefully and ask for the reference section. When you find it, wander around for a few minutes before staking a claim. You will discover that libraries are a good place to watch the human race, so get the best seat in the house. Make sure you have a clear view of the librarian's desk. When you need a rest, that's where all the comic relief takes place.

Reference books

There are a number of reference books you can consult, and they are listed in the Bibliography. I won't waste space teaching you how to use them here — the librarian will be happy to do that.

Your goal is to identify and build personalised dossiers on the companies in your chosen geographic area. Do not be judgemental about what and who they might appear to be: you are fishing for possible job openings, so cast your net wide and list them all.

Take a pad of paper, and using a separate sheet for each company, copy all the relevant company information on to that piece of paper. So that we agree on 'relevant', take a look at the example on the following page.

Here, you see the names of the company's chairman and managing director, a description of the complete lines of company services and/or products, the size of the company, and the locations of its various branches. Of course, if you find other interesting information, copy it down, by all means. For instance, you might come across information on growth or shrinkage in a particular area of a company; or you might read about recent acquisitions the company has made. Write it down.

All this information will help you shine at the interview in three different ways. Your knowledge creates a favourable impression when first meeting the company; that you made an effort is noticed. That no one else bothers is a second benefit. And third, the combination says that you respect the company,

Company Ltd
Head Office: 231 Piccadilly
              London W1V9YY
Phone: 01-246 8091
Personnel (George Wanstead, dir) 01-246 8093

MD: Gordon Blair
Chairman: Sir Geoffrey Jones
Export Sales director: David Macdonald

Company produces high performance sports
cars at its Northampton plant, supplies tooling
and key components for local assembly
overseas. Exports expanding to markets in
W. Germany, US and Middle East.

Turnover (1985) £4.5M
Profits + 11.5% from 1984

Recently acquired machine tool co in
Dusseldorf.

and therefore, by inference, the interviewer; this helps set you
apart from the herd.

All your effort has an obvious short-term value in helping you
win job offers. It also has value in the long term, because you
are building a personalised reference work of your industry/

speciality/profession that will help you throughout your career whenever you wish to make a job change.

Unfortunately, no single reference work is complete. Their very size and scope means that most are just a little out of date at publication time. Also, no single reference work lists every company. Because you don't know what company has the very best job for you, you need to research as many businesses in your area as possible, and therefore you will have to look through additional reference books.

Be sure to check any specialised guides mentioned in the Bibliography, including the *Key British Enterprises* and your local manufacturing directory.

At the end of the day, pack up and head for home. Remember on the way to purchase a map of your area, drawing pins, and small size stick-on labels for implementing the next stage of your plan.

Put your map on the wall. Attack the string to a drawing pin, stick the pin on the spot where you live, and draw concentric circles at intervals of one mile. In a short space of time, you will have defaced a perfectly good map, but you'll have a *physical* outline of your job-hunting efforts.

Next, take out the company biographies prepared at the library and write 'No 1' on the first. Find the firm's location on the map and mark it with a drawing pin. Finally, mark an adhesive label 'No 1' and attach it to the head of the pin. As you progress, a dramatic picture of your day's work appears. Each pin-filled circle is a territory that needs to be covered, and each of those pins represents a potential job.

It is likely you will be back at the library again, finishing off this reference work and preparing your curriculum vitae. The research might take a few days. Try walking to the library the next time. Not only is it cheaper (a sound reason in itself), but the exercise is very important to you. You are engaged in a battle of wits, and the healthier you are physically, the sharper you will be mentally. You need your wits about you, because there are always well-qualified people looking for the best jobs. Yet it is not the most qualified who always get the job. It is the person who is best prepared who wins every time. Job hunters who knock 'em for six at the interview are those who do the homework and preparation that a failure will not do. Do a little more walking. Do a little more research.

Newspapers

Almost everybody looking for a new job buys the newspaper and then carefully misuses it. A recent story tells of a job hunter who started by waiting for the Sunday paper to be published. He read the paper and circled six jobs. Phoned the first to find it had already been filled, and in the process, got snubbed by someone whose voice had yet to break, requesting that he write in the future and send a CV. As anything is better than facing telephone conversations like that, the job hunter didn't ring the other five companies, but took a week to write a CV that no one would read, let alone understand. Sent it to a dozen companies. Waited a week for someone to phone. Waited another week. Kicked the cat. Felt bad about that, worse about himself, and had a couple of drinks. Phone rang, someone was interested in the CV but, unfortunately, not in someone who slurred his words at lunch-time. Felt worse, stayed in bed late. Phone rings: an interview! Felt good, went to the interview. They will contact in a few days. They don't, and in the calls to them, everybody is mysteriously unavailable. The job hunter begins to feel like a blot on the landscape. This is obviously an extreme example, but the story is a little too close to the bone for many, and it illustrates the wrong way to use the paper when you're looking for a job.

Unfortunately, people usually use either the newspaper *or* reference books, but rarely both. They run the risk of ending up in the buyer's market. Not a good place to be.

While reference books give you bags of hard information about a company, they tell you little about specific job openings. Newspapers, on the other hand, tell you about specific jobs that need filling now, but give you few hard facts about the company. The two types of research should complement each other. Often you will find ads in the newspaper for companies you have already researched. What a powerful combination of information this gives you going in the door to the interview!

The correct way to use newspapers is to identify all companies that are currently recruiting. Write down the pertinent details of each particular job opening on a separate piece of paper as you did earlier with the reference books. Include the company's name, address, phone number, and contact names.

In addition to finding openings that bear your particular title, look for all the companies that need staff regularly in your field. The fact that your job is not being advertised does not mean a company is not looking for you; if a company is in a recruiting mode, a position for you might be available. In the instances when a company is active but has not been advertising specifically for your skills, write down all relevant company contact data. You could be the solution to a problem that has only just arisen, and should get in touch.

It is always a good idea to examine back issues of the newspaper. These can provide a rich source of job opportunities that remain unfilled from prior advertising efforts.

The 'hidden' jobs

The reason you *must* use a combination of reference books and advertisements is that companies tend to recruit in cycles. When you rely exclusively on newspapers, you miss those companies just about to start or just ending their cycles. This comprehensive research is the way to tap what the business press refers to as the 'hidden' job market. It is paramount that you have as broad a base as possible — people know people who have *your* special job to fill.

With the addition of all these companies to your map, you will have a glittering panorama of prospects, the beginnings of a dossier on each one, and an efficient way of finding any company's exact location. This is useful for finding your way to an interview and in evaluating the job offers coming your way.

Adequate research and preparation are the very foundation for performing well at interviews. And the more interviews you have, the more your research skills will increase; they are the first step to putting yourself in a seller's market.

Chapter 2
All Things to All People –
Packaging the Curriculum Vitae

Interviewers today are continually asking for detailed examples of your past performance. They safely assume you will do at least as well (or as poorly) on the new job as you did on the old one, and so the examples you give will seal your fate. Therefore, you need to examine your past performance in a practical manner that will ensure you handle these questions correctly.

This chapter will show you how to identify the examples from your past that will impress any interviewer. There is a special bonus: you will also get the correctly packaged information for an excellent curriculum vitae. Two birds with one stone.

CVs, of course, are important, and there are two facts you must know about them. First, you are going to need one. Second, no one will want to read it. The average interviewer has never been trained to interview effectively, probably finds the interview as uncomfortable as you do, and will do everything possible to avoid discomfort. CVs are therefore used more to screen people *out* than screen them *in*. So your CV must be all things to all people.

Another hurdle to leap is avoiding the specialisation of your skills in the CV. A cold hard fact is that the first person to see your CV is often in the personnel department. This office screens for many different jobs and cannot be expected to have an in-depth knowledge of every speciality within the company – or its jargon.

For these reasons, your CV must be easy to read and understand, short, use words that are familiar to the reader and that have universal appeal. Most important, it should portray you as a problem-solver.

While this chapter covers ways to build an effective CV, its main goal is to help you perform better at the interview. You will achieve this as you evaluate your professional skills according to the exercises. In fact, you are likely to discover skills and achievements you didn't even know you had. A few you will use in your CV (merely a preview of coming attractions); the others you will use to knock 'em for six at the interview.

How to draft your CV

A good starting point is your current or last job title. Write it down. Then jot down all the other different titles you have heard that describe this job. When you are finished, follow it with a three- or four-sentence description of your job functions. Don't think too hard about it, just do it. The titles and descriptions are not carved in stone. This written description is the beginning of the CV-building exercises. You'll be surprised at what you've written; it'll read better than you had thought.

All attributes that you discover and develop in the following exercises are valuable to an employer. You possess many desirable traits, and these exercises help to reveal and to package them.

EXERCISE 1

Re-read the written job description, then write down your most *important* duty or function. Follow this with a list of the skills or special training necessary to perform that duty. Next, list the achievements of which you are most proud in this area. It could look something like this:

Duty	Train and motivate sales staff of six.
Skills	Formal training skills. Knowledge of market and ability to make untrained sales staff productive. Ability to keep successful salespeople motivated and tied to the company.
Achievements	Reduced turnover 7 per cent; increased sales 14 per cent.

The potential employer is most interested in the achievements, those things that make you stand out from the crowd. Try to appeal to a company's interests by conservatively estimating what your achievements meant to your employer. If your achievements saved time, estimate how much. If you saved money, how much? If your achievements made money for the company, how much? Beware of exaggeration; if you were part of a team, identify your achievements as such. It will make your claims more believable and will demonstrate your ability to work with others.

Achievements, of course, differ according to your profession.

Most of life's jobs fall into one of these broad categories:

- Sales
- Management and administration
- Technical and production.

While it is usual to cite the differences between these major job functions, it is far more valuable to you to recognise what they have in common. In sales, cash volume is important. In management or administration, the parallel is time saved, which is money saved; saving money is just the same as making money for your company. In the technical and production areas, increasing production (doing more in less time) accrues exactly the same benefits to the company. Job titles may differ, yet all employees have the same opportunity to benefit their employers, and in turn, themselves.

The computer revolution of the seventies and the economic recession in the early eighties have irrevocably changed the workplace. Today, companies are doing more with less; they are leaner, have higher expectations of their employees, and plan to keep it that way. The people who get jobs and get ahead today are those with a basic understanding of business goals. And successful job candidates are those who have the best interests of the company and its profitability constantly in mind.

EXERCISE 2
This simple exercise helps you get a clear picture of your achievements. If you were to talk to your supervisor to discuss a rise, what achievements would you want to discuss? List all you can think of, quickly. Then come back and flesh out the details.

EXERCISE 3
This exercise is particularly valuable if you feel you can't see the wood for the trees.

Problem Think of a job-related problem you had to face in the last couple of years. Come on, everyone can remember a problem.

Solution Describe your solution to this problem, step by step. List everything you did.

Results Finally, consider the results of your solution, in terms that would have value to an employer: money earned or saved; time saved.

EXERCISE 4

Now, a valuable exercise that turns the absence of a negative into a positive. This one helps you look at your job in a different light and accents important but often overlooked areas that help to make you special. Begin discovering for yourself some of the key personal traits that all companies look for.

First, consider actions that if not carried out properly would affect the goal of your job. If this is difficult, remember an incompetent co-worker. What did he or she do wrong? What did he or she do differently from *competent* employees?

Now, turn the absence of these negatives into positive attributes. For example, think of the employee who never managed to get to work on time. You could honestly say that someone who *did* come to work on time every day was punctual and reliable; believed in systems and procedures; was efficiency-minded and cost- and profit-conscious.

If you have witnessed the reprimands and ultimate termination of that persistently late employee, then you will see the value of the *positive* traits in the eyes of an employer. The absence of negative traits makes you a desirable employee, but no one will know unless you tell them. On completion of the exercise, you will be able to make points about your background in a positive fashion. You will set yourself apart from others, if only because others do not understand the benefits of projecting all their positive attributes.

EXERCISE 5

Potential employers and interviewers are always interested in people who:

- Are efficiency-minded;
- Have an eye for economy;
- Follow procedures;
- Are profit-oriented.

Proceed through your work history and identify the aspects of your background that exemplify these traits. These newly discovered personal pluses will not only be woven into your CV, but will be reflected in the posture of your answers when you get to the interview.

Packaging the data

You now need to take some of this knowledge and package it in a curriculum vitae. There are three standard types of CV:

1. *Chronological.* The most frequently used format. Use it when your work history is stable and your professional growth is consistent. Avoid it if you have experienced performance problems or have made frequent job changes.
2. *Functional.* Use this type if you have been unemployed for long periods of time or have jumped jobs too frequently. A functional CV is created without employment dates or company names, and concentrates on skills and responsibilities.
3. *Prioritised.* The prioritised CV can be useful if you have changed careers, or when current responsibilities don't relate specifically to the job you want. It is written with the most relevant experience to the job you're seeking placed first.

Notice that each style is designed to minimise certain undesirable traits. As few of us are perfect (present company excepted), most people find it most effective to write a combination CV.

Employers are wary of the 'too-perfect' CV. With this in mind, there are just seven rules for creating a workmanlike one.

1. Use the most general of job titles. You are, after all, a hunter of interviews, not of specific titles. Cast your net wide. Use a title that is specific enough to put you in the field, yet vague enough to elicit further questions. A job title can be made specifically vague by adding the term 'specialist' (eg Computer Specialist, Administration Specialist, Production Specialist).
2. Avoid giving a job objective. If you must state a specific job as your goal, couch it in terms of contributions you can make in that position. Do not state what you expect of the employer.
3. Do not state your current salary. If you are earning too little or too much, you could rule yourself out before getting your foot in the door. Do not mention your desired salary for the same reason.
4. Remember that people get great joy from pleasant surprises. Show a little gold now, but let the interviewer discover the motherlode at the interview.
5. Take whatever steps are necessary to keep the CV's length to a two-page maximum. No one reads long CVs; they are boring, and every company is frightened that if it lets in a

windbag, it will never get him or her out again.

6. Your CV must be typed. As a rule of thumb, three pages of double-spaced, handwritten notes make one page of typescript.

7. Finally, emphasise your achievements and problem-solving skills. Keep the CV general.

Chapter 3

The Executive Briefing

A general curriculum vitae does have drawbacks. First, it is too general to relate your qualifications to each specific job. Second, more than one person will probably be interviewing you, and that is a major stumbling block. While you will ultimately report to one person, you may well be interviewed by other team members. When this happens, the problems begin.

A manager says, 'Spend a few minutes with this candidate and tell me what you think.' Your general CV may be impressive, but the manager rarely outlines the job being filled or the specific qualifications he or she is looking for adequately. This means that other interviewers do not have any way to qualify you fairly and specifically. While the manager will be looking for specific skills relating to projects at hand, personnel will be trying to match your skills to the job-description-manual vagaries, and the other interviewers will flounder in the dark because no one told them what to look for. This naturally could reduce your chances of landing a job offer.

Professionals in the employment services industry face this problem daily. At Dunhill we came up with a solution called the 'executive briefing'. It enables you to quickly customise your CV to each specific job, and acts as a focusing device for whoever interviews you.

Like many great ideas, the executive briefing is beautiful in its simplicity. It is a sheet of paper with the company's requirements for the job opening listed on the left side, and your skills — matching point by point the company's needs — on the right. It looks like this:

Executive Briefing

Dear Sir/Madam:

While my curriculum vitae will provide you with a general outline of my work history, my problem-solving abilities, and some achievements, I have taken the time to list your current specific requirements and my applicable skills in those areas. I hope this will enable you to use your time effectively today.

Your Requirements:	My Skills:
1. Management of public library service area (for circulation, reference, etc).	1. Experience as head reference librarian at University of Redbrick.
2. Supervision of 14 full-time support employees.	2. Supervised support staff of 17.
3. Ability to work with larger supervisory team in planning, budgeting, and policy formulating.	3. During my last year, I was responsible for budget and reformation of circulation rules.
4. ALA.	4. I have this degree.
5. Three years' experience.	5. One year with public library; two with University of Redbrick.

This briefing ensures that each CV you send out addresses the job's specific needs and that every interviewer at that company will be interviewing you for the same job.

Send an executive briefing with every CV; it will substantially increase your chances of obtaining an interview with the company. An executive briefing sent with a CV provides a comprehensive picture of a thorough professional, plus a personalised, fast, and easy-to-read synopsis that details exactly how you can help with their current needs.

The use of an executive briefing is naturally restricted to jobs that you have discovered through your own efforts or seen advertised. It is obviously not appropriate for sending when the requirements of a specific job are unavailable. However, by following the directions in the next chapter, you will be able to use it frequently and effectively.

Part 2
Getting to Square One

With the groundwork completed, you are geared up and ready to knock 'em for six. So how do you begin?

What are your choices? Read the sits vacant ads? Everybody else does. Apply for jobs listed with the unemployment office? Everybody else does. Send CVs to companies on the off-chance they have a job that fits yours? Everybody else does. Or, of course, you can wait for someone to ring you. Employ these tactics as your main thrust for hunting down the best jobs in town, and you will fail as do *thousands* of other people who fall into the trap of using such outdated job-hunting techniques.

When you look like a penguin, act like a penguin, and hide among penguins, don't be surprised if you get lost in the flock. Today's business market-place demands a different approach. Your career does not take care of itself; you must go out and grab the opportunities. Grant yourself the right to pick and choose among *many* job offers with a guaranteed approach: pick up the telephone. 'Hello, Mr Smith? My name is Martin Yate. I am an experienced training specialist...'

It's as easy as that.

Guide your destiny by speaking directly to the professionals who make their living in the same way you do. A few minutes spent phoning different companies from your research dossier, and you will have an interview. When you get one interview from making a few calls, how many do you think could be arranged with a day's concerted effort?

Because you are in control, it is possible to set your multiple interviews close together. This way your interviewing skills improve from one to the next. And soon, instead of scheduling multiple interviews, you can be weighing multiple job offers.

Chapter 4

Paint the Perfect Picture on the Phone

Before making that first, nerve-racking telephone call, you must be prepared to achieve one of these three goals. They are listed in priority order:

- I will arrange a meeting; or
- I will arrange a time to talk further on the phone; or
- I will establish a referral lead on a promising job opening elsewhere.

Always keep these goals in mind. By the time you finish the next four chapters, you'll be able to make any one of them quickly and easily.

Planning the phone call

To make the initial phone call a success, all you need to do is paint a convincing word picture of yourself. To start, remember the old saying: 'No one really listens; we are all just waiting for our turn to speak.' With this in mind, you shouldn't expect to hold anyone's attention for extended periods of time, so the picture you create needs to be brief yet thorough. Most of all, it should be 'specifically vague': specific enough to arouse interest, to make the company representative prick up his or her ears; vague enough to encourage questions, to make him or her *pursue* you. The aim is to paint a representation of your skills in broad brush strokes with examples of the money-making, money-saving, or time-saving accomplishments all companies like to hear about.

A presentation made over the telephone must possess four characteristics to be successful. These can best be remembered by an old acronym from the advertising world, AIDA.

A — You must get the company representative's *attention*.
I — You must get the company representative's *interest*.
D — You must create a *desire* to know more about you.
A — You must encourage the company representative to take *action*.

With AIDA you get noticed. The interest you generate will be displayed by questions being asked. 'How much are you making?' or, 'Do you have a degree?' or, 'How many years' experience do you have?' By giving the appropriate answers to these and other questions (which will be discussed in detail), you will change interest into a desire to meet you and convert that desire into an interview.

The types of question you are asked also enable you to identify the company's specific needs, and once they are identified, you can gear the on-going conversation towards those needs.

Here are the steps in building your AIDA presentation:

STEP 1

This covers who you are and what you do. It is planned to get the company representative's attention, to give the person a reason to stay on the phone. This introduction will include your job title and a brief generalised description of your duties and responsibilities. Use a non-specific job title, as you did for your CV. Remember: getting a foot in the door with a generalised title can provide the occasion to sell your superior skills.

Tell just enough about yourself to whet the company's appetite, and cause the representative to start asking questions. Again, keep your description a little vague. For example, if you describe yourself as simply 'experienced', the company representative *must* try to qualify your statement with a question: 'How much experience do you have?' That way, you establish a level of interest. *But*, if you describe yourself as having four years' experience, and the company is looking for seven, you are likely to be ruled out without even knowing there was a job to be filled. *Never* specify exact experience or list all your accomplishments during the initial presentation. Your aim is just to open a dialogue. Example:

> Good morning, Mr Smith. My name is Jenny Jones. I am an experienced office equipment salesperson with an indepth knowledge of the office products industry. Have I caught you at a good time?

Note. Never *ever* ask if you have caught someone at a *bad* time. You are offering them an excuse to say 'yes'. By the same token, asking whether you have caught someone at a good time will *usually* get you a 'yes'. Then you can go directly into the rest of your presentation.

STEP 2

Now you are ready to generate interest, and from that, desire; it's time to sell one or two of your accomplishments. You should already have identified these during the CV-building exercises. Pull out no more than two items and follow your introductory sentence with them. Keep them brief and to the point, without embellishments. Example:

> As the No 3 salesperson in my company, I increased sales in my territory 15 per cent to over £1 million. In the last six months, I won three major accounts from my competitors.

STEP 3

You have made the company representative want to know more about you, so now you can make him or her take action. Include the reason for your call and a request to meet. It should be carefully constructed to finish with a question that will bring a positive response, which will launch the two of you into a nuts-and-bolts discussion between two professionals. Example:

> The reason I'm calling, Mr Smith, is that I'm looking for a new challenge, and having researched your company, I felt that we might have some areas for discussion. Are these the types of skill and accomplishment you look for in your staff?

Your presentation ends with a question that guarantees a positive response, and the conversation gets moving.

Script your presentation

Your task now is to write out a presentation using these guidelines and your work experience. Knowing exactly what you are going to say and what you wish to achieve is the only way to generate multiple interviews and multiple job offers. When your presentation is prepared and written, read it aloud to yourself, and imagine the faceless company representative at the other end of the line. Practise with a friend or spouse.

After you make the actual presentation on the phone, you'll *really* begin to work on arranging a meeting, another phone conversation, or establishing a referral. There will probably be silence on the other end after your initial pitch. Be patient. The company representative needs time to digest your words. If you feel tempted to break the silence, resist; you do not want to break the person's train of thought, nor do you want the ball back in your court.

This contemplative silence may last as long as 20 seconds, but when the company representative responds, there will be only three things that can happen:

1. Company representative can agree with you and arrange a meeting.
2. Company representative can ask questions that show interest. Examples:
   • Do you have a degree?
   • How much are you earning?
   Any question, because it denotes interest, is known as a *buy signal*. And handled properly, it will enable you to arrange a meeting.
3. Company representative can raise an objection. Examples:
   • I don't need anyone like that now.
   • Send me a CV.

These objections, when handled properly, will *also* result in an interview with the company, or at least a referral to someone else who has job openings. In fact, you will frequently find that objections prove themselves to be terrific opportunities disguised as unsolvable problems.

I hope you can handle the first option with little assistance because, for obvious reasons, it doesn't get a chapter; you can go straight to Part 3. The next two chapters focus on buy signals and objections, and how to turn them into interviews.

Chapter 5

Responding to Buy Signals

With just a touch of nervous excitement you finish your presentation: 'Are these the types of skill and accomplishment you look for in your staff?' There is silence on the other end. It is broken by a question. You breathe a sigh of relief because you remember that *any* question denotes interest and is a *buy signal*.

Now conversation is a two-way street, and you are most likely to win an interview when you take responsibility for your half of the conversation. Just as the employer's questions show interest in you, your questions should show your interest in the work done at the company. By asking questions of your own in the normal course of that chat, questions usually tagged on to the end of one of your answers, you will forward the conversation. Also, these questions help you find out what particular skills and qualities are important to each different employer. Inquisitiveness will increase your knowledge of the opportunity at hand, and that knowledge will give you the power to arrange a meeting.

The alternative is to leave all the interrogation to the employer. That will place you on the defensive, and at the end of the talk, you will be as ignorant of the real job parameters as you were at the start. And the employer will know less about you than you might want him to know.

Applying the technique of giving a short answer and finishing each reply with a question will carry your call to its logical conclusion: the interviewer will tell you the job specifics, and as that happens, you will present the relevant skills or attributes. In any conversation, the person who asks the question controls its outcome. You phoned the employer to get an interview as the first step in generating a job offer, so take control of your destiny by taking control of the conversation. Example:

Jenny Jones. Good morning, Mr Smith. My name is Jenny Jones. I am an experienced office equipment salesperson with an in-depth knowledge of the office products industry.

Have I caught you at a good time?...As the No 3 sales-person in my company, I increased sales in my territory 15 per cent to over £1 million. In the last six months, I won three major accounts from my competitors. The reason I'm calling, Mr Smith, is that I'm looking for a new challenge, and having researched your company, I felt we might have areas for discussion. Are these the types of skill and accomplishment you look for in your staff?

(Pause.)

Mr Smith. Yes, they are. What type of equipment have you been selling? *(Buy signal!)*

J. My company carries a comprehensive range, and I sell both the top and bottom of the line, according to my customers' needs. I have been noticing a considerable interest in the new multi-faction machines. *(You've made it a conversation; you further it with the following...)* Has that been your experience recently?

S. Yes, especially in the colour and acetate capability machines. *(Useful information for you.)* Do you have a degree? *(Buy signal!)*

J. Yes, I do. *(Just enough information to keep the company representative chasing you.)* I understand your company prefers graduate salespeople to deal with its more sophisticated clients. *(Your research is paying off.)*

S. Our customer base is very sophisticated, and they expect certain behaviour and competence from us. *(An inkling of the kind of person they want to hire.)* How much experience do you have? *(Buy signal!)*

J. Well, I've worked both in operations and sales, so I have a wide experience base. *(General but thorough.)* How many years of experience are you looking for? *(Turning it around, but furthering the conversation.)*

S. Ideally, four or five for the position I have in mind. *(More good information.)* How many do you have? *(Buy signal!)*

J. I have two with this company, and one and a half before that. I fit right in with your needs, don't you agree? *(How can Mr Smith say no?)*

S. Uhmmm…what's your territory? *(Buy signal!)*

J. I cover the metropolitan area. Mr Smith, it really *does* sound as if we might have something to talk about. *(Remember, your first goal is the face-to-face interview.)* I am planning to take Thursday and Friday off at the end of the week. Can we meet then? *(Make Mr Smith decide what day he can see you, rather than whether he will see you at all.)* Which would be best for you?

S. How about Friday morning? Can you bring a CV?

Your conversation should proceed with this give-and-take. Your questions show interest, carry the conversation forward, and teach you more about the company's needs. By the end of the conversation you have an interview arranged and several key areas to promote when you arrive:

- Company sees growth in multi-function machines, especially those with colour and acetate capabilities
- They want business and personal sophistication
- They ideally want four or five years' experience
- They are interested in your metropolitan contacts

The above is a fairly simple scenario, and even though it is constructive, it doesn't show you the tricky signals that can spell disaster in your job hunt. They are *apparently* simple buy signals, yet in reality they are a part of every interviewer's arsenal called 'knock-out' questions — questions that can save the interviewer time by quickly ruling out certain types of candidate. Although these questions most frequently arise during the initial telephone conversation, they can crop up at the face-to-face interview; the answering techniques are applicable throughout the interview cycle.

Note. We all come from different backgrounds and geographical areas. I see and recognise these regional differences every day in my training job. So understand that while my answers cover correct approaches and responses, they do not attempt to capture the rich regional and personal flavour of conversation. You and I will never talk alike. So, don't learn the example answers parrot-fashion. Instead, you should take the essence of the responses and personalise them until the words fall easily from your lips.

Knock-out questions

Buy signal. 'How much are you making/do you want?'

This is a direct question looking for a direct answer, yet it is a knock-out question. Earning either too little or too much could ruin your chances before you're given the opportunity to shine in person. There are a number of options that could serve you better than a direct answer.

- *Put yourself above the money.* 'I'm looking for a job and a company to call home. If I am the right person for you, I'm sure you'll make me a fair offer. What is the salary range for the position?'
- *Give a vague answer.* 'In the 20s. The most important things to me are the job itself and the company. What is the salary range for the position?'
- *Or you could use a technique employed by most salespeople, and answer a question with a question.* 'How much does the job pay?' It is sometimes very effective to answer a question with a question; if you don't feel yourself to be the sales type, however, you may need to practise it.

When you are pressed a second time for an exact figure, be honest and forthright. You have to be. If it turns out to be too much, say, 'Mr Smith, my previous employers felt I am well worth the money I earn due to my skills, dedication, and honesty. Were we to meet, I'm sure I could demonstrate my value and my ability to contribute to your department. You'd like an opportunity to make that evaluation, wouldn't you?'

Notice the 'wouldn't you?' at the end of the reply. A reflexive question such as this is a great conversation-forwarding technique because it encourages a positive response. Conservative use of reflexive questions can really help you to move things along. Watch the sound of your voice, though. A reflexive question can sound pleasantly conversational or pointed and accusatory; it's a case of not *what* you say, but *how* you say it. These questions are easy to create. Just add, 'wouldn't you?', 'didn't you?', 'won't you?', couldn't you?', 'shouldn't you?', or 'don't you?' to the end of any sentence and the interviewer will almost always answer 'yes'. You have kept the conversation alive.

Repeat the reflexive questions to yourself. They have a certain rhythm that will help you remember them.

Buy signal. 'Do you have a degree?'

Always answer the exact question; beware of giving unrequested and possibly too much information. For example, if you have a bachelor's degree from East Anglia, your answer is 'Yes,' not 'Yes, I have a BA in fine arts from East Anglia.' Perhaps the company wants an architecture degree. Perhaps the company representative has bad feelings about East Anglia graduates. You don't want to be knocked out before you've been given the chance to prove yourself.

'Yes, I have a degree. What background are you looking for?'

You can always answer a question with a question. 'I have a diverse educational background. Ideally, what are you looking for?'

If a degree that you lack is required, strive to use the 'university of life' answer. For instance: 'My education was cut short by the necessity of earning a living at an early age. My past managers have found that my life experience and responsible attitude are *very* valuable assets to the department. Also, I am still continuing my education.'

Buy signal. 'How much experience do you have?'

Too much or too little could easily rule you out. Be careful how you answer and try to gain time. It is a vague question, and you have a right to ask for qualifications.

'Could you help me with that question?' or, 'Are you looking for overall experience or in some specific areas?' or, 'Which areas are most important to you?' Again, you answer a question with a question. The employer's response to this, while gaining you time, tells you what it takes to do the job and therefore what you have to say to get it, so take mental notes (you can even write them down, if you have time). Then give an appropriate response.

You might want to retain control of the conversation by asking another question, for example, 'The areas of expertise you require sound very interesting, and it sounds as if you have some exciting projects at hand. Exactly what projects would I be involved with over the first several months?'

After one or two buy signal questions are asked (apart from the ones mentioned, they contain no traps), you should ask to meet the company. If you simply ask, 'Would you like to meet me?' there are only two possible responses: yes or no. Your options are greatly lessened. However, when you intimate that you will be in the area on a particular date or dates ('I'm going to be in town on Thursday and Friday, Mr Smith. Which would be better for you?'), you have asked a question that moves the conversation along dramatically. This question gives the company representative the choice of meeting you on Thursday or Friday, rather than meeting you or not meeting you. By presuming the 'yes', you reduce the chances of hearing a negative, and increase the possibility of a face-to-face meeting.

Chapter 6

Responding to Objections

Even with the most convincing word picture, the silence may not be broken by a buy signal, but by an objection. An objection is usually a statement, not a question: 'Why don't you send me a CV,' or, 'I haven't time to see you,' or, 'I don't need anyone like you right now.'

These seem like brush-off lines, but almost all objections can be converted into interviews when handled properly. Often they are just more disguised opportunities. As this section teaches you to seize hidden opportunities successfully, notice what all your responses have in common with buy signals: they all end with a question, a question that will enable you to learn more about the reason for the objection, overcome it, and once again lead the conversation towards a face-to-face interview.

In dealing with objections, as with differences of opinion, nothing is gained by confrontation, although much is to be gained by appreciating the other person's point of view. Most objections you hear are best handled by first demonstrating your understanding of the other's viewpoint. Always start your response with 'I understand,' or, 'I can appreciate your position,' or, 'I see your point,' or, 'Of course,' followed by, 'However...' or, 'Also consider...' or a similar line that carries the conversation forward.

Remember, these responses should not be learned merely to be repeated. You need only to understand and implement their *meaning*, to understand their *concept* and put the answers in your own words. Personalise all the suggestions to your character and style of speech.

Objection. 'Why don't you send me a CV?'

Danger here. The company representative may be genuinely interested in seeing your CV as a first step in the interview cycle; or it may be a polite way of getting you off the phone. You should identify what the real reason is without causing antagonism. At the same time, you want to open up the conversation. A good reply would be: 'Of course, Mr Smith. Would you give me your exact title and the full address? ... Thank you. So that I can be sure that my qualifications fit your needs, what skills are you looking for in this position?'

Notice the steps:

- Apparent agreement to start
- A show of consideration
- A question to guide the conversation at the end.

Answering in this fashion will open up the conversation. Now, our hypothetical Mr Smith will relay the aspects of the job that are important to him. With this knowledge, you can sell Smith on your skills over the phone. Also, you will be able to draw attention to your skills in these specific areas in the future, in:

- Following conversations
- The covering letter to your CV
- The executive briefing
- Your face-to-face meeting
- Your follow-up after the meeting.

The information you glean will give you power and will increase your chances of receiving a job offer.

Objection. 'I haven't time to see you.'

If the employer is too busy to see you, he or she has a problem, and by recognising that, perhaps you can show yourself as the one to solve it. However, you should avoid confrontation; it is important that you demonstrate empathy for the speaker. Agree, empathise, and ask a question that moves the conversation forward.

'I understand how busy you must be; it sounds like the kind of atmosphere I could work well in. Perhaps I could ring you back at a better time. When are you least busy, the morning or afternoon?'

The company representative will either make time to talk now, or will arrange a better time for the two of you to talk further.

Here are three other wordings you could use for the same objection: 'Since you are so busy, what is the best time of day for you? First thing in the morning, or is the afternoon a quieter time?' or, 'I will be in your area tomorrow, so why don't I come by and see you?'

Or, of course, you can combine the two: 'I'm going to be in your part of town tomorrow, and I could drop by and see you. What is your quietest time, morning or afternoon?' By presuming the invitation to a meeting, you make it harder for the company representative to object. And if he or she is *truly* busy, your consideration will make it even harder to object.

Objection. 'You are earning too much.'

You should not have brought up salary in the first place. Go straight to gaol. If the client brought up the matter, that's a buy signal, which was discussed in the last chapter. If the job really doesn't pay enough, all you've gained is experience. Avoid confrontation on the salary question too early on. How to make a success of this seeming dead end is handled in the next chapter.

Objection. 'We only promote from within.'

Your response could be: 'I realise that, Mr Smith. Your development of employees is a major reason I want to get in! I am bright, conscientious, and need a company like yours. When you do recruit from outside, what assets are you looking for?'

The response finishes with a question designed to carry the conversation forward, and to give you a new opportunity to sell yourself. Notice that the response assumes that the company *is* recruiting from outside, even though the company representative has said otherwise. You have called his bluff, but in a professional, inoffensive manner.

Objection. 'You'll have to talk to personnel.'

Your reply is: 'Of course, Mr Smith. Whom should I speak to in personnel and what specific position should I mention?'

You cover a good deal of ground with this response. You establish whether there is a job there or whether you are being fobbed off to personnel to waste their time and your own. Also, you move the conversation forward again, and have changed the thrust of it to your advantage. Develop a specific job-related question to ask while the company representative is answering the first question. It can open a fruitful line for you to pursue. If you receive a non-specific reply, probe a little deeper. A simple phrase like, 'That's interesting, please tell me more,' or, 'Why's that?' will usually do the trick.

Or you can ask: 'When I speak to personnel, will it be about a specific job *you* have, or is it to see if I might fill a position elsewhere in the company?'

Armed with this information, you can talk to personnel about your conversation with Mr Smith. Remember to get the name of a specific person to speak with, and to quote the company representative. Example:

Good morning, Mr Johnson. Mr Smith, the regional sales manager, suggested we should speak to arrange an interview.

This way, you will show personnel that you are *not* a waste of their time; because you know someone in the company, you won't be regarded as one of the hundreds of blind callers they always get. As the most overworked, understaffed department in a company, they will appreciate that. Most important, you will stand out, be noticed.

Don't look at the personnel department as a roadblock; it may contain a host of opportunities for you. Because a large company may have many different departments that can use your talents, personnel is likely to be the only department that knows all the openings. You might be able to arrange three or four interviews with the same company for three or four different positions!

Objection. 'I really wanted someone with a degree.'

You could answer *this* by saying: 'Mr Smith, I appreciate your position. It was necessary that I start earning a living early in life. If we meet, I am certain you would recognise the value of my additional practical experience. All we would need is a short while, and I'm going to be in your area tomorrow and next week. When would be a good time for you?'

If that doesn't work, ask what the company policy is for support and encouragement of employees taking night classes, continuing education courses etc.

Objection. 'I don't need anyone like you now.'

Short of suggesting the employer fire someone to make room for you, the chances of getting an interview with this particular company are slim, but with the right question, this person will give you a personal introduction to someone else who could use your talents. Asking that right question or series of questions is what networking and the next chapter are all about. So on the occasions when the techniques for answering buy signals or rebutting objections do not get you a meeting, 'Getting Live Leads from Dead Ends' will!

Chapter 7
Getting Live Leads from Dead Ends

There will be times when you have said all the right things on the phone, but hear, 'I don't need anyone like you just now'. Not every company has a job opening for you, nor are you right for every job. There will be times when you must accept a temporary setback and understand that the rejection is not one of you as a human being. By using other interview development questions, though, you will be able to turn these occasions into job interviews.

The company representative is a professional and knows other professionals in his or her field, in other departments, subsidiaries, even other companies. If you approach the phone presentation in a professional manner, he or she, as a fellow professional, will be glad to advise you on who is looking for someone with your skills. Nearly everyone you call will be pleased to head you in the right direction, *but only if you ask!* And you'll be able to ask as many questions as you desire, because you will be recognised as a colleague intelligently using the professional network. The company representative knows also that his good turn in referring you to a friend at another company will be returned in future. And, as a general rule, companies prefer candidates to be referred this way over any other method.

But do *not* expect people to be clairvoyant. There are two sayings:

'You get what you ask for,'

and

'If you don't ask, you don't get.'

When you are sure that no job openings exist within a particular company, *ask* one of these questions:

* Who else in the company might need someone with my qualifications?
* Does your company have any other divisions or subsidiaries that might need someone with my attributes?

- Do you know anyone in the business community who might have a lead for me?
- What are the most rapidly growing companies in the area?
- Who should I speak to there?
- Do you know anyone at the Corporation Company Limited?
- When do you anticipate an opening in your company?
- Are you planning any expansion or new projects that might create an opening?
- Do you see any change in your manpower needs?

Each one of these interview development questions can gain you an introduction or lead to a fresh opportunity. The questions have not been put in any order of importance. That is for you to do. Take a sheet of paper and, looking at the list, decide what question you would ask if you had time to ask only one. Write it down. Do this with the remaining questions on the list. As you advance, a comfortable list of questions in priority order will be developed. Add questions of your own. For instance, the type of computer or word-processing equipment a company has might be important to some professions, but not to others, and a company representative might be able to lead you to companies that have your machines. Be sure that any question you add to your list is specific and leads to a job opening. Avoid questions like, 'How's business these days?' Time is valuable, and time is money to both of you. When you're satisfied with your list of interview development questions, put them on a fresh sheet of paper and store it safely with your telephone presentation and CV.

These interview development questions will lead you to a substantial number of jobs in the hidden job market. You are getting referrals from the 'in' crowd, who know who is recruiting whom long before that news is generally known, and by so doing, you establish a very effective referral network.

When you get leads on companies and specific individuals to talk to, be sure to thank your benefactor and ask to use his or her name as an introduction. The answer, you will find, will always be 'yes', but asking shows you as someone with manners and that *alone* will set you apart. You might also suggest to your contact that you leave your telephone number in case he or she comes across someone who can use you. You will be surprised how many people call back with a lead.

With personal permission to use someone's name on your

next networking call, you have been given the greatest of job-search gifts: a personal introduction. In these instances, your call will begin with:

> Hello, Mr Smith. My name is Jack Jones. Joseph McDonald recommended me to phone you. By the way, he sends his regards. *(Pause for any response to this.)* He felt we might have a useful discussion.

Follow up on every lead you get. Too many people become elated at securing themselves an interview and then cease all effort to generate additional interviews, believing a job offer is definitely on its way. Your goal is to have a choice of the best jobs, and without multiple interviews, there is no way you'll have that choice. Asking interview development questions ensures that you are tapping all the secret recesses of the hidden job market.

Networking is a continuous cycle:

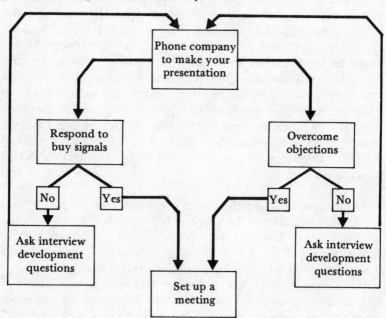

Make a commitment to sell yourself, to make telephone calls, to make a referral network, to recognise buy signals and objections for what they really are — opportunities to shine. Make a commitment to ask interview development questions at every seeming dead end: they will lead you to every job in town.

Chapter 8
The Telephone Interview

In this glorious technological age, the first contact with a potential employer is always by telephone. It's the way business is done today.

It happens in one of three ways:

- When you are networking, and the company representative goes into a screening process immediately because you have aroused his or her interest;
- A company phones unexpectedly as a result of a CV you have mailed, and catches you off-guard; or
- You or an agency you have spoken to has set up a specific time for a telephone interview.

Whatever circumstance creates this telephone interview, you must be prepared to handle the questioning and use every means at your disposal to win the real thing — the *face-to-face* meeting. The telephone interview is the trial run for the face-to-face, and is an opportunity not to be fumbled; your happiness and prosperity may hinge on it.

This, the first contact with your future employer, will test your mental preparation. Remember: you can plant in your mind any thought, any plan, desire, strategy, or purpose, and translate it into reality. Put your goal down on paper and read it aloud to yourself every day, because the constant reiteration will crystallise your aims, and that provides the most solid base of preparation.

Being prepared for a telephone interview takes organisation. You never know when a company will ring once you have started networking (the word gets around), although it is usually at the worst of times, such as 8 o'clock Monday morning when you are sleeping late, or 4.56 in the afternoon, just as you return from walking the dog. You can avoid being caught *completely* off-guard by keeping your CV and alphabetised company dossiers by the telephone.

The most obvious (and often most neglected) point to

remember is this: during the interview, the company representative has only ears with which to judge you. This is something you must overcome. Here are some tips:

□ *Take a surprise phone call in your stride.* If you receive a call as a result of a mailed CV or a telephone message you left, and you are unprepared, be calm. Sound positive, friendly, and collected:

Thank you for phoning, Mr Smith. How do you spell that? Would you wait just a moment while I close the door?

Put the phone down, take three deep breaths to slow your heart down, pull out the appropriate company dossier and your CV, put a smile on your face (it improves the timbre of your voice), and pick up the phone again. Now you are in control of yourself and the situation.

□ *Beware of over-familiarity.* You should always refer to the interviewer by his or her surname until invited to do otherwise.

□ *Allow the company representative to do most of the talking, to ask the questions.*

□ *Beware of giving yes/no answers.* They give no real information about your abilities.

□ *Be factual in your answers.* Brief yet thorough.

□ *Keep up your end of the conversation.* Don't let the interviewer do *all* the talking. Ask some questions of your own.

□ *Speak directly into the telephone.* Keep the mouthpiece about 1 inch from your mouth. Do not smoke or eat while on the phone. Numbered among the mystical properties of our telephone system is its excellence at picking up and amplifying background music and voices, especially young ones. This is only excelled by the power with which it transmits the sounds of food being chewed or smoke being inhaled or exhaled. Smokers, remember: there are no laws about discriminating against smokers, and therefore, all non-smokers naturally discriminate. They know that even if you don't smoke at the interview, you'll have been chain-smoking before and will carry the smell with you as long as you are around them. So, they won't even give you a chance to get through the door.

□ *Take notes.* They will be invaluable to you in preparing for the face-to-face meeting.

If, for any reason, the company representative is interrupted, jot down the topic under discussion. When he or she gets back on the line, you helpfully recap: 'We were just discussing...' This will be appreciated, and will set you apart from the others.

The company representative may talk about the organisation, and from the dossier in front of you, you will also know facts about the set-up. A little flattery goes a long way: admire the company's achievements and you are, in fact, admiring the interviewer. Likewise, if any areas of common interest arise, comment on them, and agree with the interviewer when it is possible; people engage people like themselves.

If the interviewer does not give you the openings you need to sell yourself, be ready to salvage the situation and turn it to your advantage. Have a few work-related questions prepared (eg 'What exactly will be the three major responsibilities in this job?' or, 'Would I be using a personal computer?'). While you are getting the explanation, wait for a pause so that you can tell the interviewer your appropriate skills: 'Would it be of value if I described my experience in the area of office management?' or, 'Then my experience in word processing should be a great help to you.' Under no circumstances, though, should you ask about the money you want, or benefits and holidays; that comes later.

Remember that your single objective at this point is to sell yourself and your skills; if you don't do that, you may never get the face-to-face interview.

The telephone interview has come to an end when you are asked whether you have any questions. Ask any more questions that will improve your understanding of the job requirements. If you haven't asked before, now is the time to establish what projects you would be working on in the first six months. By discovering them now, you will have time before the face-to-face meeting to package your skills to the needs at hand, and to create the appropriate executive briefing.

And if you have not already asked or been invited to meet the interviewer, now is the time. Take the initiative.

'It sounds like a very interesting opportunity, Ms/Mr Smith, and a situation where I could definitely make a contribution. The most pressing question I have now is, when can we meet?' (*Note*. Even though the emphasis throughout has been on putting things in your own words, *do* use 'make a contribution'. It shows pride in your work – a key personal trait.)

Once the details are confirmed, finish with this request: 'If I need any additional information before the interview, I would like to feel free to get back to you.' The company representative will naturally agree. No matter how many questions you get answered in the initial conversation, there will always be something you forget. This allows you to phone again to satisfy any curiosity and will also enable you to increase rapport. Don't take *too* much advantage of this, though. One well-placed phone call that contains two or three considered questions will be appreciated; four or five phone calls will not.

Taking care to ascertain the correct spelling and pronunciation of the interviewer's name shows your concern for the small but important things in life: it *will* be noticed. This is also a good time to establish who else will be interviewing you, their titles and how long the meeting is expected to last. Follow with a casual enquiry as to what direction the meeting will take.

'Would you tell me some of the critical areas we will discuss on Thursday?' you might ask. The knowledge gained will go a long way in packaging yourself and will allow you time to brush up any weak or rusty areas.

It is difficult to evaluate an opportunity properly over the telephone. Even if the job doesn't sound right, go to the interview. It will give you practice, and the job may look better when you have more facts. You might even discover a more suitable opening when you go to the face-to-face interview.

Chapter 9
The Curtain Goes Up

Backstage in the theatre, the announcement, 'Places, please', is made five minutes before the curtain goes up. This is the performers' signal to psyche themselves up, complete final costume adjustments, and make time to reach the stage. They are getting ready to go on stage and knock 'em dead. You should go through a similar process.

Winning that job offer depends not only on the things you do well, but also on the absence of things you do poorly. As the interview date approaches, settle down with your CV and the exercises you performed in building it. Immerse yourself in your past successes and strengths. This is a time for building confidence. A little nervousness is perfectly natural and healthy, but channel the extra energy in a positive direction by beginning your physical and mental preparations. First, you should assemble your interview kit. It will include:

☐ *The company dossier.*

☐ *Two or three copies of your curriculum vitae, all but one for the interviewer.* It is perfectly all right to have it in front of you at the interview; it shows you are organised. It also makes a great cheat sheet (after all, the interviewer is using it for that reason) and it can be kept on your lap during the interview with pad and pencil. It is not unusual to hear, 'Mr Jones wasn't made an offer because he didn't pay attention to detail and could not even remember his employment dates.' And those are just the kinds of thing you are likely to forget in the heat of the moment.

☐ *A pad of paper and writing instruments.* These articles have a twofold purpose. They demonstrate your organisation and interest in the job; they also give you something constructive to do with your hands during the interview. Bring along a blue or black pen for filling in applications.

☐ *Contact telephone numbers.* If you get detained on the way to the interview, you can ring and let the company representative know.

□ *Take the sensible precaution of gathering reference letters from your employers, just in case.*

□ *A list of job-related questions.* During the interview is the time when you gather information to evaluate a job (the actual evaluation comes when you have an offer in hand). At the end of the interview, you will be given the opportunity to ask additional questions. Develop some that help you understand the job's parameters and potential. You might ask:

- Why is the job open?
- Where does the job lead?
- What is the job's relationship to other departments?
- How do the job and the department relate to corporate aims?

Now you have a little more work to do:

□ *Gather any additional information you can about the company or the job.* If time permits, ask the interviewer's secretary to send you some company literature. Absorb whatever you can.

□ *Make sure you have directions for reaching the venue.* Decide on your form of transport and finalise your time of departure. Check the route, distance, and travel time. Write all this down legibly and put it with the rest of your interview kit. If you forget to verify date, time, and place, you might not even arrive at the right place, or on the right day, for your interview.

Personal appearance

First impressions are the strongest you make, and they are based on your appearance. There is only one way to dress for the first meeting: clean-cut and conservative. You may or may not see yourself this way, but how you see yourself is not important now; your only concern is how others see you. As you could be asked to appear for an interview at a scant couple of hours' notice, you must be in a constant state of readiness. Keep your best two suits of clothing freshly cleaned, shirts ironed, and shoes polished. Never wear these outfits unless you are interviewing. Here are some more tips:

- Regardless of sex or hairstyle, have your hair trimmed once a month.

- Keep jewellery to a minimum. A wedding or signet ring is acceptable, of course.
- While a shower or bath prior to an interview is most desirable, the wearing of aftershave or perfume is most decidedly not. You are trying to be appointed, not dated.
- You should never drink alcohol the day before an interview. It affects eyes, skin, and your wits.
- Nails should be trimmed and manicured at all times, even if you work with your hands.

For women:

- Wear a suit or a dress with a jacket. Do not wear a trouser suit or jeans.
- If you carry a briefcase, don't carry a handbag as well. You may meet a number of people and will have trouble juggling your luggage to shake hands.
- Wear low heels. Spike heels make you wobble and are regarded by many as inappropriate in the workplace.
- Avoid linen; it fatigues too easily.
- Stay away from everything low-cut, tight, or diaphanous.

For men:

- Avoid loud colours and anything that has been faddish...
- ...such as that dayglo tie. A 2½ to 2¾ inch tie is *de rigueur*. Patterns should be paisley or foulard. Avoid anything wider unless you are applying for a job as a carpet salesman.
- Blue or grey for suits primarily. White for shirts is always safest.
- Black shoes with plain socks.

The way you dress, the way you look to a potential employer at the first interview, tells him or her how you feel about yourself. It also portrays how seriously you take both the interview and the interviewer.

Arrival

To arrive at an interview too early indicates over-anxiousness; to arrive late is inconsiderate. The only sensible solution is to arrive at the interview on time, but at the location early. This allows you time to visit the wash room and make the necessary adjustments to your appearance. Take a couple of minutes in this temporary sanctuary to perform your final mental preparations:

- Review the company dossier.
- Recall the positive things you will say about past employers.
- Breathe deeply and slowly for a minute. This will dispel your natural physical tension.
- Repeat to yourself that the interview will be a success and afterwards the company representatives will wonder how they ever managed without you.
- Smile and head for the interview.

Under no circumstances back out because you do not like the receptionist or the look of the office; that would be allowing interview nerves to get the better of you. As you are shown into the office, you are on!

This potential new employer wants an aggressive and dynamic employee, but someone who is less aggressive and dynamic than themselves, so take your lead from the interviewer.

Do:

- Give a firm handshake; once is enough.
- Make eye contact and smile. Say, 'Hello, Ms Smith. I am John Jones. I have been looking forward to meeting you.'

Do not:

- Use first names (unless asked).
- Smoke (even if invited).
- Sit down (until invited).
- Show anxiety or boredom.
- Look at your watch.
- Discuss equal rights, sex, race, national origin, religion, age.
- Show samples of your work (unless requested).
- Ask about benefits, salary, holidays.
- Assume a submissive role; treat the interviewer with respect, but as an equal.

Now you are ready for anything. Except for the tough questions that are going to be thrown at you next.

Part 3
Great Answers to the Toughest Questions

'Like being on trial for your life' is how many people look at a job interview. They are probably right. With the interviewer as judge and jury, you are at least on trial for your livelihood. Therefore, you must lay the foundation for a winning defence. F Lee Bailey, America's most celebrated defence lawyer, attributes his success in the court-room to preparation. He likens himself to a magician going into court with 50 rabbits in his hat, not knowing which one he'll really need, and ready to pull out any single one. Bailey is successful because he is ready for any eventuality. He takes the time to analyse every situation and every possible option. He never underestimates his opposition. He is always prepared. F Lee Bailey usually wins.

Another famous lawyer, Louis Nizer, successfully defended *all* of his 50-plus capital charge clients. When praised as the greatest court-room performer of his day, Nizer denied the accolade. He claimed for himself the distinction of being the *best prepared*.

You won't win your day in court just based on your skills. As competition for the best jobs increases, employers are comparing more and more applicants for every opening and asking more and more questions. To win against stiff competition, you need more than just your merits. When the race is close, the final winner is often as not picked for a comparative lack of negatives when ranged against the other contenders. Like Bailey and Nizer, you can prove to yourself that the job always goes to the best prepared.

During an interview, employers ask you dozens of searching questions: questions that test your confidence, poise, and desirable personality traits. Questions that trick you into contradicting yourself, and questions that probe your quick thinking and job skills. They are all designed so that the interviewer can make decisions in four critical areas:

- Can you do the job?

- Do you fit the company image?
- Will you complement or disrupt the department?
- Is the money right?

Notice that only one of the critical areas has anything to do with your professional skills. Being able to do the job is only part-way to getting an offer. Whether you will fit in and make a contribution is just as important to the interviewer. Those traits the company probes for during the interview are the same that will mark a person for professional growth when on board. In this era of high unemployment and high specialisation, companies become more critical in the selection process and look more actively for certain traits, some of which cannot be ascertained by a direct question or answer. Consequently, the interviewer will seek a pattern in your replies that shows your possession of these traits.

The time spent in 'court' on trial for your livelihood contains four deadly traps:

- Failure to listen to the question.
- Annoying the interviewer by answering a question that was not asked.
- Providing superfluous information (keep answers brief, thorough, and to the point).
- Attempting to interview without preparation.

The effect of these blunders is cumulative, and each reduces your chances of receiving a job offer.

The number of offers you win in your search for the ideal job depends on your ability to answer a staggering array of questions in terms that have value and relevance to the employer: 'Why do you want to work here?' or, 'What are your biggest accomplishments?' or, 'How long will it take you to make a contribution?' or, 'Why should I take you on?' or, 'What can you do for us that someone else cannot do?' or, 'What is your greatest weakness?' or, 'Why aren't you earning more?' or, 'What interests you least about this job?' are just *some* of the questions you will be asked.

The specimen answers in the following chapters come from across the job spectrum. While the specimen answer might come from the mouth of an administrator — and you are a salesperson — the common denominator of all job functions in contributing to the bottom line will help you draw the parallel to *your* job.

You will also notice that each of the specimen answers teaches a small, yet valuable lesson in good business behaviour; something you can use both to get the job and to make a good impression when you are on board.

And remember, the answers provided in the following chapters should not be repeated word for word, exactly as they come off the page. *You* have your own style of speech (not to mention your own kind of business experience), so try to put the answers in your *own* words.

Chapter 10

How to Knock 'em for Six

Can you answer all these questions off the top of your head? Can you do it in a way that will set your worth above the other job candidates? I doubt it; they were *designed* to catch you off guard. But they won't after you have read this book.

Even if you could answer some of them, it would not be enough to assure you of victory: the employer is looking for certain intangible assets as well. Think back to your last job for a moment. Can you recall someone with fewer skills, less professionalism, and less dedication who somehow leveraged his or her career into a position of superiority to yours? He or she was able to do this only by cleverly projecting a series of personality traits that are universally sought by all successful companies. Building these key traits into your answers to the interviewer's questions will win you any job and set the stage for your career growth at the new company.

There are 20 key personality traits; they are the passport to your success at an interview. Use them for reference as you customise your answers to this chapter's tough questions.

Personal profile

Personal profile keys are searched for by the interviewer to determine what type of person you *really* are. The presence of these keys in your answers tells the company representative how you feel about yourself, your chosen career, and what you will be like to work with. Few of these keys will arise from direct questions. Your future employer will be searching for them in your answers to specific job performance probes. The following words and phrases are those you will project as part of your successful, healthy personal profile:

- *Drive*. A desire to get things done. Goal-oriented.

- *Motivation*. Enthusiasm and a willingness to ask questions. A company realises that a motivated person accepts added challenges and does that little bit extra on every job.

- *Communication skills.* More than ever, the ability to talk and write effectively to people at all levels in a company is a key to success.

- *Chemistry.* The company representative is looking for someone who does not get rattled, wears a smile, is confident without self-importance, gets along with others; who is, in short, a team player.

- *Energy.* Someone who always gives that extra effort in the little things as well as important matters.

- *Determination.* Someone who does not back off when a problem or situation gets tough.

- *Confidence.* Not braggadocio. Poise. Friendly, honest, and open with all employees high or low. Neither intimidated by the top brass, nor overly familiar.

Professional profile

All companies seek employees who respect their profession and their employer. Projecting these professional traits will identify you as loyal, reliable, and trustworthy:

- *Reliability.* Following up on yourself, not relying on anyone else to ensure the job is well done, and keeping management informed every step of the way.

- *Honesty/Integrity.* Taking responsibility for your actions, both good and bad. Always making decisions in the best interests of the company, never on whim or personal preference.

- *Pride.* Pride in a job well done. Always taking the extra step to make sure the job is done to the best of your ability. Paying attention to the details.

- *Dedication.* Whatever it takes in time and effort to see a project through to completion, on deadline.

- *Analytical skills.* Weighing the pros and cons. Not jumping at the first solution to a problem that presents itself. The short- and long-term benefits of a solution against all its possible negatives.

- *Listening skills.* Listening and understanding, as opposed to waiting your turn to speak.

Achievement profile

I mentioned earlier that companies have very limited interests: making money, saving money (the same as making money), and saving time, which does both. Projecting your achievement profile, in however humble a fashion, is the key to winning any job.

- *Money saved.* Every penny saved by your thought and efficiency is a penny earned for the company.

- *Time saved.* Every moment saved by your thought and efficiency enables your company to save money and make more in the additional time available. Double bonus.

- *Money earned.* Generating revenue is the goal of every company.

Business profile

Projecting your business profile is important on those occasions when you cannot demonstrate ways you have made money, saved money, or saved time for previous employers. These keys demonstrate you are always on the look-out for opportunities to contribute, and that you keep your boss informed when an opportunity arises.

- *Efficiency.* Always keeping an eye open for wastage of time, effort, resources, and money.

- *Economy.* Most problems have two solutions: an expensive one, and one that the company would prefer to implement.

- *Procedures.* Procedures exist to keep the company profitable. Don't work around them. This also means keeping your boss informed. You tell your boss about problems or good ideas, not his or her boss. Follow the chain of command. Do not implement your own 'improved' procedures or organise others to do so.

- *Profit.* The reason all the above traits are so universally admired in the business world is because they relate to profit.

Stress how your qualifications match the job requirements

As the requirements of the job are unfolded for you at the interview, meet them point by point with your qualifications. If your experience is limited, stress the key profile traits, your relevant interests, and desire to learn. If you are weak in just one particular area, keep your mouth shut; perhaps that dimension will not arise. If the area is probed, be prepared to handle and overcome the negative by stressing additional complementary skills that compensate.

Do not show discouragement if the interview appears to be going poorly. You have nothing to gain by showing defeat, and it could merely be an interview tactic to test your self-confidence.

If for any reason you get flustered or lost, keep a straight face and posture; gain time to marshal your thoughts by asking, 'Could you help me with that?' or, 'Would you repeat that?' or, 'That's a good question; I want to be sure I understand. Could you please explain that again?'

The tough questions

Now it is time for you to study the tough questions. Use the examples and explanations to build answers that promote your background and skills.

□ *What are the reasons for your success in this profession?*

With this question, the interviewer is not interested in examples of your success — he wants to know what makes you tick. Keep your answers short, general, and to the point. Using your work experience, personalise and use value keys from your personal profile, professional profile, and business profile. For example, 'I attribute my success to three reasons: the support I've always received from co-workers, which always encourages me to be cooperative and look at my specific job in terms of what we as a department are trying to achieve. This gives me great pride in my work and its contribution to the department's efforts. Finally, I find that every job has its problems, and while there's always a costly solution, there's usually an economical one as well, whether it's in terms of time or money.'

□ *What is your energy level like? Describe a typical day.*

You must demonstrate good use of your time, that you believe in planning your day beforehand, and that when it is over, you review your own performance to make sure you are reaching the desired goals. No one wants a part-time employee, so you should sell your energy level. For example, your answer might end up with: 'At the end of the day when I'm ready to go, I make a rule always to type one more letter [make one more call etc], and clear my desk for the next day.'

☐ *Why do you want to work here?*

To answer this question, you must have researched the company and built a dossier. Your research work from Chapter 1 is now rewarded. You should reply with the company's attributes as you see them. Cap your answer with reference to your belief that this can provide you with a stable and happy work environment — the interviewer's company has that reputation — and that such an atmosphere would encourage your best work.

'I'm not looking for just a pay cheque. I enjoy my work and am proud of my profession. Your company produces a superior product. I think that gives us certain things in common, and means I would fit in well with your team.'

☐ *What kind of experience do you have for this job?*

This is a golden opportunity to sell yourself, but before you do, be sure you know what is most critical to the interviewer. The interviewer is not just looking for a competent engineer, typist, or salesperson; he or she is looking for someone who can contribute quickly to the current projects. When interviewing, companies invariably give everyone a broad picture of the job, but the person they hire will be a problem-solver, someone who can contribute to the specific projects in the first six months. Only by asking will you identify the areas of your interviewer's greatest urgency and therefore interest.

If you do not know the projects you will be involved with in the first six months, you must ask. Level-headedness and analytical ability are respected, and you will naturally answer the question more appropriately. For example, a company experiencing slippage problems might appreciate this answer: 'My high-speed machining background and familiarity with your equipment will allow me to contribute quickly. I understand deadlines, delivery schedules, and the importance of getting the product despatched quickly. Finally, my awareness of economy and profit has always kept reject parts to a bare minimum.'

☐ *Are you willing to go where the company sends you?*

Unfortunately, with this one you are, as the saying goes, 'damned if you do and damned if you don't'. What is the *real* question? Do they want you to relocate or just travel on business? If you simply answer 'no', you will not get the job offer, but if you answer 'yes', you could end up in John o'Groats. So play for time and ask, 'Are you talking about business travel, or is the company relocating?' In the final analysis, your answer should be 'yes'. You don't have to accept the job, but without the offer you have no decision to make. Your single goal at an interview is to sell yourself and win a job offer. Never forget, only when you have the offer is there a decision to make about that particular job.

☐ *What did you like/dislike about your last job?*

Most interviews start with a preamble by the interviewer about his company. Pay attention: this information will help you answer the question. In fact, any statement the interviewer makes about the job or corporation can be used to your advantage.

So in answer, you liked everything about your last job. You might even say your company taught you the importance of certain keys from the business profile, achievement profile, or professional profile. Criticising a prior employer is a warning flag that you could be a problem employee. No one intentionally takes trouble on board, and that is what's behind the question. Keep your answers short and positive. You are only allowed one negative about past employers, and only then if your interviewer has a 'hot button' about his department or company; if so, you will have written it down on your notepad, in which case the only thing your past employer could not offer was, for example: 'The ability to contribute more in different areas in the smaller environment you have here. I really liked everything about the job. The reason I want to leave is to find a position where I can make a greater contribution. You see, I work for a big company that is encouraging increasing specialisation of skills. The smaller environment you have here will, as I said, allow me to contribute far more in different areas.' Tell them what they want to hear; replay the hot button.

Of course, if you interview with a large company, turn it around. 'I work for a small company and don't get the time to specialise in one or two major areas . . .' Then replay the hot button.

☐ *How do you feel about your progress to date?*

This question is not geared solely to rate your progress; it also rates your self-esteem (personal profile keys). Be positive, yet do not give the impression you have already done your best work. Make the interviewer believe you see each day as an opportunity to learn and contribute, and that you see the environment at this company as conducive to your best efforts.

'Given the parameters of my job, my progress has been excellent. I know the work and understand the importance of the role it plays within my company's operations. I feel I am just reaching that point in my career when I can make significant contributions.'

☐ *How long would you stay with the company?*

The interviewer might be thinking of offering you a job. So you must encourage him or her to sell you on the job. With a tricky question like this, end your answer with a question of your own that really puts the ball back in the interviewer's court. Your reply might be: 'I would really like to settle down with this company. I take direction well and enjoy learning. As long as I am growing professionally, there is no reason for me to make a move. How long do you think I would be happy here?'

☐ *Have you done the best work you are capable of doing?*

Say 'yes', and the interviewer will think you're a has-been. As with all these questions, personalise your work history and include the essence of this reply: 'I'm proud of my professional achievements to date, but I believe the best is yet to come. I am always motivated to give my best efforts, and in this job there are always opportunities to contribute when you stay alert.'

☐ *How long would it take you to make a contribution to our company?*

Again, be sure to qualify the question. In what area does the interviewer need rapid contributions? You are best advised to answer this question with a question: 'That is an excellent question. To help me answer, what do you anticipate my responsibilities will be for the first six or seven months?' You give yourself time to think while the interviewer concentrates on images of you working for the company. When your time comes to answer, start with: 'Let's say I started on Monday the 17th. It will take me a few weeks to settle down and learn the ropes. I'll be earning my keep very quickly, but making a real contribution...*(hesitant pause)*...Do you have a special project in mind you will want me to get involved with?' This response could lead directly to a job offer, but if not, you already have the interviewer thinking of you as an employee.

☐ *What would you like to be doing five years from now?*

The safest answer contains a desire to be regarded as a true professional and team player. As far as promotion is concerned, that depends on finding a manager with whom you can grow. Of course, you will ask what opportunities exist within the company before being any more specific: 'From what I know and what you have told me about the growth here, it seems that manufacturing is where the heavy emphasis is going to be. It seems that's where you need the effort and where I could contribute most towards the company's goals.'

☐ *What are your qualifications?*

Again you need to qualify the question. Does the interviewer want job-related or academic qualifications? Ask. If he or she is looking for job qualifications, you need to know exactly the work you'll be doing in the first few months. Again, notice the importance of understanding the current projects and therefore the problems that need to be tackled. Ask. Then use appropriate value keys from all four categories tied in with relevant skills and achievements. You might say: 'I can give you a general answer, but I feel my answer might be more valuable if you could tell me about specific work assignments in the early months...'

Or: 'If the major task right now is reducing the reject ratio, I should tell you this. I work in a high-speed manufacturing environment, and since I've been there, I've reduced rejects by 26 per cent...'

☐ *What are your biggest accomplishments?*

Keep your answers job-related; from earlier exercises, a number of achievements should spring to mind. If you exaggerate contributions to major projects, you will be accused of suffering from 'coffee machine syndrome', the affliction of a junior clerk who claimed success for an Apollo space mission based on his relationships with certain scientists, established at the coffee machine. You might begin your reply with: 'Although I feel my biggest achievements are still ahead of me, I am proud of my involvement with...I made my contribution as part of that team and learned a lot in the process. We did it with hard work, concentration, and an eye for the bottom line.'

□ *Can you work under pressure?*

You might be tempted to give a simple yes or no answer, but don't. It reveals nothing and you lose the opportunity to sell your skills and value profiles. Actually, this common question often comes from an unskilled interviewer, because it is closed-ended. As such, it does not give you the chance to elaborate. Whenever you are asked one of these, mentally add: 'Please give me a brief yet comprehensive answer.' Do this, and you will give the information requested and seize an opportunity to sell yourself. For example, you could say: 'Yes, I usually find it stimulating. However, I believe in planning and proper management of my time to reduce panic deadlines within my area of responsibility.'

□ *What is your greatest strength?*

Key to your background and build in a couple of the key value profiles from different categories. You will want to demonstrate pride, reliability, ability to stick with a difficult task yet change courses rapidly when required. You can rearrange the previous answer here. Your answer in part might be: 'I believe in planning and proper management of my time. And yet I can still work under pressure.'

□ *What interests you most about this job?*

Be straightforward, unless you haven't been given adequate information to determine an answer, in which case you should ask a question of your own to clarify. Perhaps you could say, 'Before I answer, could you tell me a little more about the role this job plays in the departmental goals?' or, 'Where is the biggest vacuum in your department at the moment?' The additional information you gather with these questions provides the appropriate slant to your answer: that is, what is of greatest benefit to the department and to the company. Careerwise, this obviously has the greatest benefit to you, too. Your answer then displays the personality traits that support the existing need. Your answer in part might include: 'I'm looking for a challenge and an opportunity to make a contribution, so if you feel the biggest challenge in the department is...I'm the one for the job.' Then include the personality traits that support your statements. Perhaps: 'I like a challenge, my background demonstrates excellent problem-solving abilities, and I always see a project through to the finish.'

□ *How much money do you want?*

This is a knock-out question; give the wrong answer, and you will immediately be eliminated. It is always a temptation to ask for the moon knowing you can come down, but that is a poor approach. Companies have strict salary ranges (called salary curves) for every job, so an ill-considered answer can reduce your job-offer chances to zero. The solution? You need the best offer possible without pricing yourself out of the market, so it's time to dance: 'I naturally want to make as much as my background and experience permit. I was/am making x pounds a year. The most important thing to me, however, is the job and the people I will be working with. If I am right for the job, and I believe I am, I feel sure you'll make me a fair offer.' You may tag a question on to the end of this response: 'What figure did you have in mind?'

□ *What are you looking for in your next job?*

You want a company where your personal profile keys and professional profile keys will allow you to contribute to business value keys. Avoid saying what you want the company to give you; you must say what you want in terms of what *you* can give to your employer. The key word in the following example is 'contribution': 'My experience at the XYZ Company has shown me I have a talent for motivating people. This is demonstrated by my team's absenteeism dropping 20 per cent, turnover steadying at 10 per cent, and production increasing 12 per cent. I am looking for an opportunity to continue that kind of contribution, and a company and supervisor who will help me develop in a professional manner.'

□ *Why should I hire you?*

Your answer will be short and to the point. It will highlight areas from your background that relate to current needs and problems. Recap the interviewer's description of the job, meeting it point by point with your skills. Finish your answer with: 'I have qualifications, I'm a team player, I take direction, and have the desire to make a thorough success.

□ *What can you do for us that someone else cannot do?*

This question will come only after a full explanation of the job has been given. Recap the interviewer's job description, then follow with: 'I can bring to this job a determination to see projects through to a proper conclusion. I listen and take direction well. I am analytical and don't jump to conclusions. And finally, I understand we are in business to make a profit, so I keep an eye on cost and return. How do these qualifications fit your needs?'

You finish with a question that asks for feedback or a powerful answer. If you haven't covered the interviewer's hot buttons, he or she will cover them now, and you can respond accordingly.

☐ *Describe a difficult problem you've had to deal with.*

This is a favourite tough question. It is designed to probe your professional profile; specifically, your analytical skills: 'Well, I always follow a five-step format with a difficult problem. One, I stand back and examine the problem. Two, I recognise the problem as the symptom of other, perhaps hidden, factors. Three, I make a list of possible solutions to the problem. Four, I weigh both the consequences and cost of each solution, and determine the best solution. And five, I go to my boss, outline the problem, make my recommendation, and ask for my superior's advice and approval.'

Then give an example of a problem and your solution. For example: 'When I joined my present company, I filled the shoes of a manager who had been fired. Staff turnover was very high. My job was to reduce the turnover, improve morale, and increase sales. Sales of our new copier had slumped for the fourth quarter in a row. The new employer was very concerned, and he even gave me permission to clean house. The cause of the problem? The sales team had never had any sales training. All my people needed was an intensive sales training course. My boss gave me permission to join the Institute of Training and Development, which cost £55. With what I learned there, I turned the department around. Sales continued to slump in my first quarter. Then they skyrocketed. Management was pleased with the sales, my boss was pleased because the solution was effective and cheap. I only had to replace two salespeople.'

☐ *What have you learned from jobs you have held?*

Tie your answer to your business and professional profile. The interviewer needs to understand that you seek and can accept constructive advice, and that your business decisions are based on the ultimate good of the company, not your personal whim or preference. 'More than anything, I have learned that what is good for the company is good for me. So I listen very carefully to directions and always keep my boss informed of my actions.'

The profiles you have projected in this answer are:

- Listening skills (professional profile)
- Your concern for the bottom line (business profile)
- Your willingness to follow procedures (business profile).

☐ *What would your references say?*

You have nothing to lose by being positive. If you demonstrate how well you and your boss got along, the interviewer does not have to ask, 'What do you dislike about your current manager?'

The higher up the corporate ladder you climb, the more likely it is that references will be checked. It is a good idea to ask past employers to give you a letter of recommendation. This way you know what is being said. It reduces the chances of the company representative checking up on you, and if you are asked this question you can pull out a sheaf of rousing accolades and hand them over.

☐ *What type of decisions did you make on your last job?*

Your answer should include reference to the fact that your decisions were all based on appropriate business profile keys. The interviewer may be searching to define your responsibilities or he or she may want to know that you don't overstep yourself. It is also an opportunity, however humble your position, to show your achievement profile.

For example: 'Being in charge of the post room, I am responsible for making sure people get information without delay. The job is well defined, and my decisions aren't that difficult. I noticed a year or two ago that when I took the mail around at 10am, everything stopped for 20 minutes. I had an idea and gave it to my boss. She got it cleared by the director, and ever since, we take the mail around just before lunch. Mr Gray, the director, thinks my idea improved productivity and saved time.'

☐ *Why were you dismissed?*

This is a *very* difficult question to answer, because you have to overcome the stigma of having your employment terminated. Looking at that painful event objectively, you will probably find the cause of your dismissal rooted in the absence of one or more of the 20 profiles. The fact that you were dismissed also creates instant doubt in the mind of the interviewer, and greatly increases the chances of your references being checked.

Whatever you do, don't advertise the fact that you were dismissed. If you are asked, be honest, but make sure you have packaged the reason in the best light possible. Perhaps: 'I'm sorry to say, but I deserved it. I was having some personal problems at the time and I let them affect my work. I was late arriving at work and lost my motivation. My supervisor — who, by the way, I still speak to — had directions to trim the work-force anyway, and as I was taken on only a couple of years ago, I was *one* of the first to go.'

If you can find out the employee turnover figures, voluntary or otherwise, you might add: 'Fifteen other people have left so far this year.' A combination answer of this nature minimises the stigma. You have even managed to demonstrate that you take responsibility for your actions, which shows your analytical and listening skills. If one of your past managers will speak well of you, there is nothing to lose and everything to gain by finishing with: 'Jill Johnson, at the company, would be a good person to check for a reference on what I have told you.'

Of course, being made redundant for circumstances outside your control (plant shutdown, for example) is perfectly acceptable, and should be explained in a forthright manner.

☐ *In your last job, what were some of the things you spent most of your time on, and why?*

Employees come in two categories: goal-oriented (those who want to get the job done), and task-oriented (those who believe in 'busy' work). You must demonstrate good time management, and that you are, therefore, goal-oriented, for that is what this question probes.

You might reply: 'I work on the telephone like a lot of business-people; meetings also take up a great deal of time. What is more important to me is effective time management. I find more gets achieved in a shorter time if a meeting is scheduled, say, immediately before lunch or at the close of business. I try to allocate my time in the morning and afternoon for major tasks, so I don't get bogged down in 'busy' work. At 4 o'clock, I review what I've achieved, what went right or wrong, and plan adjustments and my main thrust of business for tomorrow.'

☐ *In what ways has your job prepared you to take on greater responsibility?*

This is one of the most important questions you will have to answer. The interviewer is looking for examples of your professional growth, so you must tell a story that demonstrates it. The following example shows growth, listening skills, honesty, and adherence to procedures. Parts of it can be adapted to your personal experience. Notice the 'then and now' aspect of the answer.

'In the early days my boss would brief me morning and evening. I made some mistakes, learned a lot, and got the jobs in on time. Nowadays, I meet her every Monday morning only to discuss any major directional changes.'

Chapter 11

Negatives and Tricks

These awful-sounding questions are thrown in to test your poise, to see how you react under pressure, and to plumb the depths of your confidence. Many people ruin their chances by reacting to these questions as personal insults rather than the challenge and opportunity to shine that they *really* represent.

These trick questions can be turned to your advantage or merely avoided by nifty footwork. Either way, you will be among a select few who understand this line of questioning.

Remember with these questions to build a personalised answer that reflects your experience and profession. Practise them aloud; by doing this, your responses to these interview gambits will become part of you. This enhancement of your mental attitude will positively affect your confidence during an interview.

Especially in this chapter, reflexive questions will be very useful. Negative or trick questions are designed to sort out the steadfast players from those who wilt under pressure. Used with discretion, the reflexives will prove to the interviewer that you are able to function under pressure, and you put the ball back in the interviewer's court.

□ *I'm not sure you're suitable for the job*

The interviewer's 'I'm not sure' *really* means, 'I'd like to take you on, so here's a wide open opportunity to sell yourself to me.' He or she is probing three areas from your personal profile: your confidence, determination, and listening profiles. Remain calm mentally and physically. Put the ball straight back into the interviewer's court: 'Why do you say that?' You need both the information and time to think up an appropriate reply, but it is important to show that you are not intimidated. Work out a programme of action for this question; even if the interviewer's point regarding your skills is valid, come back with value keys and alternative compatible skills. You counter with other skills that show your competence and learning ability, and use them to show you can pick up the new skills quickly. Tie the two together and demonstrate that with your other attributes you can bring many pluses to the job. Finish your answer with a reflexive question that encourages a 'yes' answer.

'I admit my programming skills in that language are a little light. However, all programming languages have similarities. My experience demonstrates that with a competence in four other languages, getting up to speed with this one will take only a short while, also I can bring a depth of other experience to the job, wouldn't you agree?'

If the reason for the question is not a lack of technical skills, it must be a question about one of your key profile areas. Perhaps the interviewer will say, 'You haven't convinced me of your determination.' This is an invitation to sell yourself, so tell a story that demonstrates determination.

For example: 'It's interesting you should say that. My present boss *is* convinced of my determination. About a year ago we were having some problems with a union organisation in the plant. Management's problem was our 50 per cent Gujarati monolingual production workforce. Despite the fact that our people had the best working conditions and benefits in the area, they were strongly pro-union. If they were successful, we would be the first unionised division in the company. No one in management spoke the language. I took a crash course, two hours at home every night for five weeks. Then I got one of the maintenance crew to help me with my grammar and diction. Then a number of other production workers started saying simple things to me in Gujarati and helping me with the answers. I opened the first meeting with the workforce to discuss the problems, and my greeting in their own language drew an appreciative murmur. We had demonstrated that we cared enough to try to communicate. Our division never did unionise, and my determination to take the extra step paid off and allowed my superiors to negotiate from a position of caring and strength. Wouldn't you agree that shows determination?'

□ *What is your greatest weakness?*

This is a direct invitation to put your head in a noose. Decline the invitation. Your best chance is to give a generalised answer that takes advantage of value keys. Design the answer so that your 'weakness' is ultimately a positive characteristic. For example: 'I enjoy my work and always give each project my best efforts. So when sometimes I don't feel others are pulling their weight, I find it a little frustrating. I am aware of this weakness, and in these situations I try to overcome it with a positive attitude that I hope will catch on.'

Congratulations, you have just turned a bear of a question into an opportunity to sell yourself with your professional profile.

□ *Wouldn't you feel better off in another company?*

Answer 'no' and explain why. All the interviewer wants to see is how much you know about the company and how determined you are to join its ranks. Your earlier research and knowledge of personal profile keys (determination) will pay off again. Overcome the objection with an example, and show how this will help you contribute to the company; end with a question of your own. In this instance, the question has a twofold purpose: one, to identify a critical area to sell yourself; and two, to encourage the interviewer to consider an image of you working at the company.

You could reply: 'Not at all. My whole experience has been with small companies. I am good at my job and in time could become a big fish in a little pond. But that is not what I want. This corporation is a leader in its business. You have a strong reputation for encouraging skills development in your employees. This is the type of environment I want to work in. Now, coming from a small company, I have done a little bit of everything. That means that no matter what you throw at me, I will learn it quickly. For example, what would be the first project I would be involved with?'

□ *What kind of decisions are most difficult for you?*

You are human, admit it, but be careful what you admit. If you have ever had to dismiss someone, you are in luck, because no one likes to do that and the experience will stand you in good stead. Emphasise that having reached a logical conclusion, you act. If you are not in management, tie your answer to key profiles: 'It's not that I have difficulty making decisions, yet some require more consideration than others. A small example might be holiday time. Now, everyone is entitled to it, but I don't believe you should leave your boss in a quandary at short notice. I consider very carefully at the beginning of the year when I'd like to take my annual leave, and then think of alternative dates. I go to my supervisor, tell him what I hope to do, and see whether there is any conflict. I wouldn't want to be out of the office for the two weeks prior to a project deadline, for instance. So by carefully considering things far enough in advance, I don't procrastinate, and I make sure my plans fit in with my boss's schedule and the department.'

Here you take a trick question and use it to demonstrate your consideration, analytical abilities, concern for the department, and for the company bottom line.

☐ *Why were you out of work for so long?*

You must have a sound explanation for any and all gaps in your employment history. If not, you are unlikely to receive a job offer. Tell the truth; everyone understands it. Emphasise that you were not just looking for another pay cheque. You are looking for a company to settle with and make a long-term contribution to.

'Well, I enjoy my work too much just to accept the first job that came up, so I determined that the next job I took would be one where I could settle down and do my best to make a solid contribution. From everything I have heard about this company, you are a group that expects everybody to pull their weight, because you've got a real job to do. I like that, and I would like to be part of the team. What have I got to do to get the job?'

Answer the question. Compliment the interviewer and move the emphasis: from you being unemployed to how you can get the job offer.

☐ *Why aren't you earning more at your age?*

Accept this as a compliment to your skills and accomplishments. 'I have always felt that solid experience would stand me in good stead in the long run and that earnings would come in due course. Also, I am not the type of person to change jobs just for the money. At this point, I have a solid background that is worth something to a company.' Now, to avoid the interviewer putting you on the spot again, finish with a question: 'How much *should* I be earning now?' The figure could be your offer.

☐ *Why have you changed jobs so frequently?*

If you have jumped around, blame it on youth (even the interviewer was young once). Now you realise what a mistake your job hopping was, and with your added domestic responsibilities you are now much more settled. Or you may wish to impress on the interviewer that your job-jumping was never the result of poor performance, and that you grew professionally as a result of each job change.

You could reply: 'My first job involved long daily travel. I soon realised that, but I knew it would give me good experience in a very competitive field. Subsequently, I found a job much closer to home where the journey was only an hour each way. I was very happy at my second job. However, I got an opportunity to really broaden my experience with a new company that was starting up. With the wisdom of hindsight, I realise that was a mistake; it took me six months to realise I couldn't make a contribution there. I've been with my current company a reasonable length of time, so I have broad experience in different environments. I didn't *just* job hop. And you see, I have more experience than the average person of my years. Now I want to settle down and make all my diverse background pay off in my contribution to my new employer. I certainly have an idea of what the competition is up to, wouldn't you agree?'

☐ *Why do you want to leave your current job?* or, *Why did you leave your last job?*

This is a common trick question. You *should* have an acceptable reason for leaving every job you have held, but if you don't, pick one of the six acceptable reasons from the employment industry formula, CLAMPS:

C for *challenge*. You weren't able to grow professionally in that position.
L for *location*. The journey was unreasonably long.
A for *advancement*. There was nowhere for you to go. You had the talent, but there were too many people ahead of you.
M for *money*. You were underpaid for your skills and contribution.
P for *pride* or *prestige*. You wanted to be with a better company.
S for *security*. The company was not stable.

'My last company was a family-owned affair. I had gone as far as I was able. It just seemed time for me to join a more prestigious company and accept greater challenges.'

☐ *What interests you least about this job?*

This question is potentially explosive, but easily defused. Regardless of your occupation, there is at least one repetitive, mindless duty that everyone groans about and which goes with the territory. Use that as your example in a statement of this nature:

81

'Filing is probably the least demanding part of the job. However, it is important to the overall success of my department, so I try to do it with a smile.' You understand that it is necessary to take the rough with the smooth in any job.

☐ *What was there about your last company that you didn't particularly like or agree with?*

You are being checked out as a potential fly in the ointment. If you *have* to answer, it might be the way the company policies and/or directives were sometimes consciously misunderstood by some employees who disregard the bottom-line profitability of the corporation.

Or: 'You know how it is sometimes with a big company. People lose awareness of the cost of things. There never seemed to be much concern about economy or efficiency. Everyone wanted his or her year-end bonus, but only worried about it in December. The rest of the year, nobody gave a hoot. I think that's the kind of thing we could be aware of most every day, don't you agree?'

☐ *What do you feel is a satisfactory attendance record?*

There are two answers to this question: one if you are in management, one if you are not. As a manager: 'I believe attendance is a matter of management, motivation, and psychology. Letting the employees know you expect their best efforts and won't accept half-baked excuses is one thing. The other is to keep your employees motivated by a congenial work environment and the challenge of stretching themselves. Giving people pride in their work has a lot to do with it, too.'

If you are not in management, the answer is even easier: 'I've never really considered it; I work for a living, I enjoy my job, and I'm rarely sick.'

☐ *What is your general impression of your last company?*

Always answer 'very good'. Keep your real feelings to yourself, whatever they might be. There is a strong belief among the management fraternity that people who complain about past employers will cause problems for their new ones. Your answer is 'very good' or 'excellent'. Then shut up.

☐ *What are some of the problems you encounter in doing your job, and what do you do about them?*

Note well the old saying, 'A poor workman blames his tools.'

Your awareness that careless mistakes cost the company good money means you are always on the look-out for potential problems. Give an example of a problem you recognised and solved.

For example: 'My job is fairly repetitive, so it's easy to over-look problems. Lots of people do. However, I always look for them; it helps to keep me alert and motivated, so I do a better job. To give you an example, we make computer memory disks. Each one has to be machined by hand, and once completed, the slightest abrasion will turn one into a reject. I have a steady staff and little turnover, and everyone wears cotton gloves to handle the disks. Yet about six months ago, the reject rate suddenly went through the roof. Is that the kind of problem you mean? Well, the cause was one that could have gone unnoticed for ages. Jill, the section head who inspects all the disks, had lost a lot of weight, her diamond ring slipped around her finger, and it was scratching the disks as she passed them and stacked them to be despatched. Our main client was giving us a big problem over it, so my looking for problems and paying attention to detail really paid off.'

The interviewer was trying to get you to reveal weak points: you avoided this trap.

☐ *What are some of the things you find difficult to do? Why do you feel this way?*

This is a variation on a couple of earlier questions. Remember, anything that goes against the best interests of your employer is difficult to do. If you are pressed for a job function you find difficult, answer in the past tense; that way, you show that you recognise the difficulty, but that you obviously handle it well.

'That's a tough question. There are so many things that are difficult to learn in our business, if you want to do the job right. I used to have 40 clients to sell to every month, and I was so busy keeping in touch with all of them, I never got a chance to do any selling. So I graded them into three groups: the top 20 per cent whom I did business with, I called on every three weeks. The next group were those I sold to occasionally; these I called on once a month, but with a difference. Each month, I marked 10 of them to spend time with and really get to know. I still have difficulty reaching all 40 of my clients in a month, but my sales have tripled, and are still climbing.'

□ *Jobs have pluses and minuses. What were some of the minuses on your last job?*

A variation on the question, 'What interests you least about this job?' which was handled earlier. Use the same type of answer. For example, 'Like any salesperson, I enjoy selling, not doing the paperwork. But as I cannot expect the customer to get the goods, and me get my commission without it, I grin and bear it. Besides, if I don't do the paperwork, that holds up other people in the company.'

If you are not in sales, use the sales force as a scapegoat. 'In credit control, it's my job to get the money in to provide the payroll and good things like that. Half the time, the goods are despatched before I get the paperwork because sales says, "It's a rush order." That's a real minus to me. It was so bad at my last company, we tried a new approach. We talked it over with sales and explained our problem. The result was that incremental commissions were based on cash in, not on invoice date. They saw the connection, and things are much better now.'

□ *What kind of people do you like to work with?*

This is the easy part of a tricky three-part question. Obviously: people who have pride, honesty, integrity, and dedication to their work. Now...

□ *What kind of people do you find it difficult to work with?*

The second part of the same question. You could say: 'People who don't follow procedures, or slackers. The occasional rotten apples who don't really care about the quality of their work. They're long on complaints, but short on solutions.' And the third part of the question...

□ *How have you successfully worked with this difficult type of person?*

This is the most difficult part of the three-part question. To this you might reply: 'I stick to my guns, keep enthusiastic, and hope some of it will rub off. I had a big problem with one fellow; all he did was complain — and always in my area. Eventually, I told him how I felt. I said if I were a millionaire, I'd have all the answers and wouldn't have to work, but as it was, I wasn't, and had to work for a living. I told George that I really enjoyed his company, but I didn't want to hear it any more. Every time I saw him after that, I presented him with a work problem and asked his advice.'

You can go on that sometimes you've noticed that such people simply lack enthusiasm and confidence, and that energetic and cheerful co-workers can often change this. 'It got him involved with something constructive, instead of just moaning.'

□ *How did you get your last job?*

The interviewer is looking for initiative. If you can, show it. At the least, show determination.

'I was actually turned down for my last job as having too little experience. I asked the manager to give me a trial before he offered it to anyone else. I went in and asked for a list of companies they'd never sold to, picked up the phone, and in that hour I arranged two appointments. How did I get the job? In a word, determination.'

If you are asked and successfully handle these trick and negatively phrased questions, the interviewer will be looking at you favourably. You may well expect next a series of questions that will tell the interviewer how you will behave once on the job: 'What kind of person are you *really*, Mr Jones?'

Chapter 12

What Kind of Person Are You *Really*, Mr Jones?

Will you reduce your new employer's life expectancy? The interviewer wants to know! If you are offered the job and accept, you will be working together 48 weeks of the year. Every employer wants to know whether you will fit in with the rest of the staff, whether you are a team player, and most of all, whether you are manageable.

There are a number of questions the interviewer might use to probe this area. They will mainly be geared to your behaviour and attitudes in the past. Remember, it is universally believed that your past actions predict your future behaviour.

☐ *How do you take direction?*

This is really two questions. 'How do you take direction?' and 'How do you take criticism?' Your answer will cover both points. 'I take direction well and believe there are two types: carefully explained direction, when my boss has time to treat me with honour and respect; then there is the other — a brusque order or correction. While most people get upset with this, personally I always believe the manager is troubled with bigger problems and a tight schedule. As such I take the direction and get on with the job without taking offence so my boss can get on with her job. It's the only way.'

☐ *Would you like to have your boss's job?*

It is a rare boss who wants his or her livelihood taken. On my very first interview, my future boss said, 'Mr Yate, it has been a pleasure to meet you. However, until you walked in I wasn't looking for a new job. Don't you feel you would be better off with another company?'

By the same token, ambition is admired, but mainly by the ambitious. Be cautiously optimistic. Perhaps: 'Well, if my boss were promoted over the coming years, I hope to have made a strong enough contribution to warrant his recommendation. And I realise there are more skills I have to learn. That's why

I'm looking for a fresh opportunity. I'm looking for a manager who will help me develop my capabilities and grow with him.'

□ *What do you think of your current/last boss?*

Short, sweet, and shut up. People who complain about their employers are recognised to be the same people who cause the most disruption in the department. Being asked this question means the interviewer has no desire to take on trouble. 'I liked her as a person, respected her professionally, and appreciated her guidance.' This question is often followed by one that tries to validate your answer.

□ *Describe a situation where your work or an idea was criticised?*

A doubly dangerous question. You are being asked to say how you handle criticism and to detail your faults. If you are asked this question, describe a poor *idea* that was criticised, *not* poor work. Poor work can cost money and is a warning sign, obviously, to the interviewer.

One of the wonderful things about a new job is that you can leave the past entirely behind, so it does not matter how you handled criticism in the past. What does matter is how the interviewer would *like* you to handle criticism, if and when it becomes his or her unpleasant duty to dish it out; that's what the question is really about. So relate one of those 'it-seemed-like-a-good-idea-at-the-time' anecdotes, and finish with how you handled the criticism. You could say: 'I listened carefully and resisted the temptation to interrupt or defend myself. Then I fed back what I heard to make sure the facts were straight. I asked for advice, we bounced some ideas around, then I came back later and represented the idea in a more viable format. My supervisor's input was invaluable.'

□ *Tell me about yourself*

This is not an invitation to ramble on. You need to know more about the question before giving an answer. 'What area of my background would be most interesting to you?' This will help the interviewer help you with the appropriate focus, so you can avoid discussing irrelevancies. Never answer this question without finding out whether the interviewer wishes to hear about your business or personal life. However the interviewer responds to your qualifying question, the tale you tell should demonstrate one or more of the 20 key personality profiles. Perhaps honesty, integrity, being a team player, or determination. If you choose 'team player', part of your answer might include this: 'I put my heart into everything I do, whether it be sports or work. I find that getting along with your peers and being part of the team makes life more enjoyable and productive.'

☐ *What have you done that shows initiative?*

The question probes whether you are a 'doer', someone who will look for ways to increase sales, save time, or save money. The kind of person who gives a manager a pleasant surprise once in a while, who makes life easier for co-workers. Do beware, however, that your example of initiative does not show a disregard for company policies and procedures.

'My boss has to organise a lot of meetings. That means developing agendas, letting employees around the country know the dates well in advance, getting materials printed, etc. Most people in my position sit and wait for the work to be given them. I don't. Every quarter I sit down with my boss and find out the dates of all his meetings for the next six months. I immediately make the hotel and travel arrangements and then work backwards. I ask myself questions like, "If the agenda for the July meeting is to reach the field at least six weeks beforehand, when must it be finished by?" Then I come up with a deadline. I do this for all the major activities for all the meetings. I put the deadlines in his diary; and mine, only two weeks earlier. That way I remind the boss that the deadline is getting closer. My boss is the best organised, most relaxed manager in the company. None of his colleagues can understand how he does it.'

☐ *What are some of the things about which you and your supervisor disagreed?*

It is safest to state that you did not disagree.

☐ *In what areas do you feel your supervisor could have done a better job?*

The same goes for this one. No one admires the wisdom of hindsight.

You could reply: 'I have always had the highest respect for my supervisor. I have always been so busy learning from Mr Jones that I don't think he could have done a better job. He has really brought me to the point where I am ready for greater challenges. That's why I'm here.'

☐ *What are some of the things your supervisor did that you disliked?*

If you and the interviewer are both non-smokers, for example, and your boss isn't, use it. Apart from that: 'You know, I've never thought of our relationship in terms of like or dislike. I've always thought our role was to get along together and get the job done.'

☐ *How well do you feel your boss rated your job performance?*

This is one very sound reason to ask for written evaluations of your work before leaving a company. Instead of answering, you whip out the citations.

Many performance review procedures include an evaluation of your ability to accept greater challenge; perhaps yours do. If you *don't* have written references, perhaps: 'My supervisor always rated my job performance well. In fact, I was always rated as being capable of accepting further responsibilities. The problem was there was nothing available in the company, that's why I'm here.'

☐ *How interested are you in sport?*

A recently completed survey of US middle- and upper-management personnel found that the executives who listed group sports/activities among their leisure activities made an average of £2,000 per year *more* than their sedentary colleagues. Don't you just love football, suddenly? The interviewer is looking for your involvement in groups, as a signal that you know how to get along with others and pull together as a team.

'I really enjoy most team sports. Don't get a lot of time to indulge myself, but I am a regular member of my company's cricket team.' Apart from team sports, endurance sports are seen as a sign of determination: swimming, running, and cycling are all acceptable.

☐ *What personal characteristics are necessary for success in your field?*

You know the answer to this one: it's a brief recital of key personality profiles.

You might say: 'To be successful in my field? Drive, motivation, energy, confidence, determination, good communication, and analytical skills. Combined, of course, with the ability to work with others.'

☐ *Do you prefer working with others or alone?*

This question is usually used to determine whether you are a team player. However, before answering be sure you know whether the job *requires* you to work alone. Then answer appropriately. Perhaps: 'I'm quite happy working alone when necessary. I don't need much constant reassurance. But I prefer to work in a group. So much more gets achieved when people pull together.'

☐ *Tell me a story*

Wow. What on earth does the interviewer mean by that question? You don't know until you get him or her to elaborate. Ask, 'What would you like me to tell you a story about?' Any other response is to risk making a fool of yourself. Very often the question is asked to see how analytical you are: people who answer the question without finding out more show that they do not think things through carefully. The subsequent question will be about either your personal or professional life. If it is about your personal life, tell a story that shows you like people and are determined. Do *not* discuss your love life. If the subsequent question is about your professional life, it might be:

☐ *What have your other jobs taught you?*

By all means, talk about the skills you have learned. Many interviewees have had success finishing their answer with: 'There are two general things I have learned from past jobs. The first is: if you are confused, ask. It's better to ask a naive question than make a stupid mistake. The second is: it is better to promise less and produce more.'

☐ *Define cooperation.*

The question asks you to explain how to function as a team player in the workplace. Your answer could be: 'Cooperation is a person's ability to sacrifice personal wishes and beliefs whenever necessary to ensure the department reaches its goals. It is also a person's desire to be part of a team, and by hard work and goodwill make the department greater than the sum of its parts.'

☐ *What difficulties do you have tolerating people with different backgrounds and interests from yours?*

Another 'team player' question with the awkward inference that you *do* have problems. Give the following answer: 'I don't have *any*.'

Now if you think the interview is only tough for the interviewee, it's time to take a look at the other side of the desk.

Chapter 13

The Other Side of the Desk

There are two terrible places to be during an interview: sitting in front of the desk wondering what on earth is going to happen next, and sitting behind the desk asking the questions. The average interviewer dreads the meeting almost as much as the interviewee, yet for opposite reasons.

Business frequently yields to the mistaken belief that any person, on being promoted into the ranks of management, becomes mystically endowed with all necessary managerial skills. This is a fallacy. Comparatively few management people have been taught to interview; most just bumble along and pick up a certain proficiency over a period of time.

There are two distinct types of interviewers who can spell disaster for you if you are unprepared. One is the highly skilled interviewer who has been trained in systematic techniques for probing your past for all the facts and evaluating your potential. The other is the totally incompetent interviewer who may even lack the ability to phrase a question adequately.

The structured interview

Skilful interviewers know exactly what they want to discover. They have taken exhaustive steps to learn the strategies that will help them to appoint only the best for their company. They follow a set format for the interview process to ensure objectivity in selection and a set sequence of questions to ensure the facts are gathered. This type of interviewer will definitely test your mettle.

There are many ways for a manager to build and conduct a structured interview, but all have the same goals:

- To ensure a systematic coverage of your work history and applicable job-related skills
- To provide a technique for gathering all the relevant facts
- To provide a uniform strategy that objectively evaluates all job candidates.

Someone using structured interview techniques will usually follow a standard format. The interview will begin with a small talk and a brief introduction to relax you. Following close on the heels of this chit-chat comes a statement geared to assure you that baring your faults is the best way to get the job. Your interviewer will then outline the steps in the interview. This will include your giving a chronological description of your work history, and then the interviewer asking some questions about your experience. Then, prior to the close of the interview, you will be given an opportunity to ask your own questions.

Sounds pretty simple, huh? Well, watch out! The skilled interviewer knows exactly what questions will be asked, why, in what order, and what the desired responses are. Every applicant for the job will be interviewed and evaluated in exactly the same fashion. You are up against a pro.

Like the hunter who learns to think like his prey, the best way to win over this interviewer is to *think* like the interviewer. In fact, take the process a little further in subtlety: you must win, but you don't want the others to realise you beat them at their own game. To do this, you must learn how the interviewer has prepared for you; and by going through the same process you will beat your competitors for the job offer.

The dangerous part of this type of interview is called 'skills evaluation'. The interviewer has analysed all the different skills it takes to do the job, and all the personality traits that complement those skills. Armed with this data, he or she has developed a series of carefully sequenced questions to draw out your relative merits and weaknesses.

Graphically, it looks like the diagram overleaf. Letters A-F are the separate skills necessary to do the job; numbers 1-20 are questions asked to identify and verify that particular skill.

This is where many of the tough questions will arise. The only way to prepare effectively is to take the interviewer's viewpoint and complete this exercise in its entirety:

- Look at the position you seek. What role does it play in helping the company achieve its corporate mission and make a profit?
- What are the five most important duties of that job?
- From a management viewpoint, what are the skills and attributes necessary to perform each of these tasks?

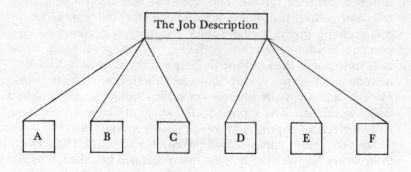

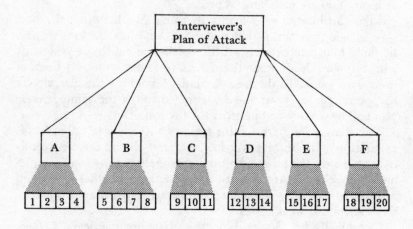

Write all this down. This exercise requires a degree of objectivity, but it will generate multiple job offers.

Now put yourself in the interviewer's shoes. What topics would you examine to find out whether a person can really do the job? If for some reason you get stuck in this process, just use your past experience. You have worked with good and bad people. Their work habits and skills will lead you to develop both the potential questions and the correct answers.

Each job skill you identify is fertile ground for the interviewer's questions. Don't forget the intangible skills that are so important to many jobs, like self-confidence or creativity, because the interviewer won't. Develop a number of questions for each job skill you identify.

Again looking back at co-workers (and still wearing the manager's mask), what are the personal characteristics that would make life comfortable or uncomfortable for you as a manager? These are also dimensions that are likely to be probed by the interviewer. Once you have identified the questions you would ask in the manager's position, the answers should come easily.

This is the way managers are trained to develop structured interview questions; I just gave you the inside track. Complete the exercise by developing the answers you would like to hear as a manager. Take time to complete the exercise conscientiously, writing out both the questions and appropriate answers.

The professional interviewer

These sharks have some juicy questions to probe your skills, attitude, and personality. Would you like to hear some of them? Notice that all the questions in this section lay out a problem, but in no way lead you to the answer. They are all two-part questions, and some are three. The additional question that can be tagged on to them *all* is, 'What did you learn from this experience?' Assume this is included whenever you get one of these questions; you'll be able to sell different aspects of your success profile.

☐ *You have been given a project that requires you to interact with different levels within the company. How do you do this? What levels are you most comfortable with?*

This is a two-part question that probes your self-confidence. The first part asks how you interact with superiors and how you motivate those working for you on the project. The second part of the question is saying, 'Tell me who you regard as your peer group; help me to pigeonhole and categorise you.' To cover these bases you will want to include the essence of this: 'There are basically two types of people I would interact with on a project of this nature. Those I report to, who bear ultimate responsibility for its success. With them I determine deadlines and how they will evaluate the success of the project. I outline my approach, breaking the project down into component parts, getting approval on both the approach and costs. I would keep my supervisors up to date on a regular basis, and seek input whenever needed. My supervisors would expect three things from me: the facts, an analysis of potential problems, and that I not be intimidated, as this could jeopardise the project's success. I would comfortably satisfy all these expectations.

'The other people to interact with in a project like this are those who work with me and for me. With these people I would outline the project and explain how successful completion will benefit the company. I would assign the component parts to those best suited to each, arrange follow-up times to assure completion by deadline. My role here would be to direct, motivate, and bring the different personalities together to form a team.

'As to comfort level, I find this type of approach enables me to interact comfortably with all levels and types of people.'

☐ *Tell me about an event that really challenged you. How did you meet the challenge? In what way was your approach different from the others?*

This is a straightforward two-part question. The first part probes your problem-solving abilities. The second asks you to set yourself apart from the herd. First of all, outline the problem. The blacker you make the situation look, the better. Having done this, go ahead and explain your solution, its value to your employer, and how it was different from other approaches.

'My company is a sales organisation; I was responsible for 70 sales offices across the country. My job was to visit each office once a year, build market strategies with management, and train and motivate the sales force. Then the recession hit. The need to service the sales force was still there, but we couldn't justify the travel cost.

'Morale was an especially important factor; you can't let the sales force feel defeated. I reapportioned my reduced budget and did the following: I dramatically increased my telephone contact with the offices. I instituted a monthly sales technique letter — how to prospect for new clients, how to negotiate difficult sales, etc. I bought and rented sales training and motivational tapes and sent them to my managers with instructions on how to use them in a sales meeting. I stopped visiting all the offices. Instead, I scheduled weekend training meetings in central locations throughout my area: one day of sales training and one day of management training — how to run sales meetings, early termination of low producers, etc.

'While my colleagues complained about the drop in sales, mine increased, albeit a modest 6 per cent. After six months my approach was officially adopted by the company.

□ *Give me an example of a method of working you have used. How did you feel about it?*

You have a choice of giving an example of either good or bad work habits. Give a good example, one that demonstrates your understanding of corporate goals, your organisational skills, analytical ability, or time management skills.

You could say: 'I believe in giving an honest day's work for a day's pay. That requires organisation and time management. I do my paperwork at the end of each day, when I review the day's achievements; with this done, I plan for tomorrow. When I come to work in the morning, I'm ready to get going without wasting time. I try to schedule meetings shortly before lunch; people get to the point more quickly if it's in their own time. I feel this is a most efficient and organised method of working.'

□ *When you joined your last company and met the group for the first time, how did you feel? How did you get on with them?*

Your answer should include, 'I naturally felt a little nervous, but I was excited about the new job. I shared that excitement with my new friends, told them that I was enthusiastic about learning new skills from them. I was open and friendly, and when given the opportunity to help someone myself, I jumped at it.'

□ *In your last job, how did you plan to interview?*

That's an easy one. Just give a description of how the skilled interviewer prepares.

□ *What would you do when you had a decision to make and no procedure existed?*

This question probes your analytical skills, integrity, and dedication. Most of all, the interviewer is testing your reaction to the 'company way of doing things'. You need to cover that with: 'I would only act without supervisor's direction if the situation was urgent and the supervisor was not available. Then I would take command of the situation, make a decision, and implement it. I would update my boss at the earliest opportunity.' If possible, tell a story to illustrate.

There are two questions that every skilled interviewer will use, especially if you are giving good answers. They will look for 'negative balance'. It will happen like this:

□ *Miss Jones, that is an excellent answer. Now to give me a balanced view, can you give me an example that didn't work out so well?*

97

With this question you are required to give an example of inadequacy. The trick is to pull something from the past, not the present, and to finish with what you learned from the experience. For example: 'That's easy. When I first joined the workforce, I didn't really understand the importance of systems and procedures. There was one time when I was too anxious to contribute and didn't have the full picture. Everyone had to fill in a report form after visiting a customer. I always put a lot of effort into it until I realised it was never read; just went in the files. So I stopped doing it for a few days to see if it made any difference. I thought I was gaining time to make more sales for the company. I was so proud of my extra sales calls I told the boss at the end of the week. My boss explained that the records were for the long term, so that should my job change, the next salesperson would have the benefit of a full client history. It was a long time ago, but I have *never* forgotten the lesson: there's always a reason for systems and procedures. I've had the best-kept records in the company ever since.'

Then the skilled interviewer will look for 'negative confirmation' by saying, 'Thank you, now can you give me another example?' The interviewer is trying to confirm a weakness. If you help, you could well do yourself out of a job.

Your reaction is this: you sit deep in thought for a good 10 seconds, then look up and say *firmly:* 'No, that's the only occasion when anything like that happened.' Shut up and refuse to be further enticed.

The incompetent interviewer

Now you should be ready for almost anything a professional interviewer could throw at you. Your foresight and strategic planning will generate multiple offers of employment for you in all circumstances except one, and that's when you face the unconsciously incompetent interviewer. This one circumstance is probably more dangerous to your job-offer status than everything else combined.

This problem is embodied in the experienced manager who is a poor interviewer, but does not know it. This person, consciously or otherwise, bases recruiting decisions on 'experience', 'knowledge of mankind' and 'gut feeling'. He or she is an unconscious incompetent. You have probably been interviewed by one in your time. Remember leaving an interview and, upon reflection, feeling the interviewer knew absolutely nothing about you or your skills? If so, you know how frustrating that can be. Here, you'll see how to turn this difficult situation to your advantage. In the future, good managers who are poor interviewers will be offering you jobs with far greater frequency than ever before. Understand that a poor interviewer can be a wonderful manager; interviewing skills are learned, not inherited or created as a result of a mystical corporate blessing.

The unconscious incompetents abound. Their heinous crime can only be exceeded by your inability *to recognise and take advantage of* the proffered opportunity.

As in handling the skilled interviewer, it is necessary to imagine how the unconscious incompetent thinks and feels.

There are many manifestations of the poor interviewer. After each example, follow instructions for appropriate handling of the unique problems each type poses for you.

Example 1. The interviewer's desk is cluttered, and the CV or application that was handed to him or her a few minutes before cannot be found.
Response. Sit quietly through the bumbling and search. Check the surroundings. Breathe deeply and slowly to calm any natural interview nerves. As you bring your adrenalin under control, you do the same thing to the interviewer and the interview. This first example is usually the most common sign of the unconscious incompetent.

Example 2. The interviewer experiences constant interruptions from the telephone or people walking into the office.
Response. This provides good opportunities for selling yourself. Make a note on your pad of where you were in the conversation and refresh the interviewer on the point when you start talking again. He or she will be impressed with your level head and good memory. These interruptions also give time, perhaps, to find something of common interest in the office, something you can compliment. You will also have time to compose the suitable value key follow-up to the point made in the conversation prior to the interruption.

Example 3. This is the interviewer who starts with an explanation of why you are both sitting there, and then allows the conversation to degenerate into a lengthy diatribe about the company.
Response. Show interest in the company and the conversation. Sit straight, look attentive (the other applicants probably fall asleep), make appreciative murmurs, and nod at the appropriate

99

times until there is a pause. When this occurs, comment that this background of the company is much appreciated, because you can now see more clearly how the job fits into the general scheme of things; that you see, for example, how valuable communication skills would be for the job. Could the interviewer please tell you some of the other job requirements? Then, as the job's functions are described, you can interject appropriate information about your background with: 'Would it be of value, Mr Smith, if I described my experience with...?'

Example 4. In this example, the interviewer begins with, or quickly breaks into, the drawbacks of the job. The job may even be described in totally negative terms. This is often done without giving a balanced view of the duties and expectations of the position.

Response. An initial negative description invariably means the interviewer has had bad experiences with staff for this position. Your course is to *empathise* (not sympathise) with his bad experiences and make it known that you recognise the importance of (for example) *reliability*, especially in this particular type of job. (You will invariably find in these instances that what your interviewer has lacked in the past is someone with a serious understanding of value keys.) Illustrate your proficiency in this particular aspect of your profession with a short example from your work history. Finish your statements by asking the company representative what are some of the biggest problems to be handled in this job. The questions demonstrate your understanding, and the interviewer's answers outline the areas from your background and skills to which you should draw attention.

Example 5. The interviewer will spend considerable time early in the interview describing 'the type of people we *are* here at Company Limited'.

Response. Very simple. You have always wanted to work for a company with this atmosphere. It creates the type of work environment that is conducive to a person really giving his or her best efforts.

Example 6. The interviewer will ask you closed-ended questions. These questions demand no more than a yes/no answer (eg 'Do you pay attention to detail?'). These questions are hardly adequate to establish your skills, yet you must handle them effectively to secure the job offer.

Response. A yes/no answer to a closed-ended question will not get you that offer. The trick is to treat each closed-ended question as if the company representative has added, 'Please give me a brief yet thorough answer.' Closed-ended questions are often mingled with statements followed by pauses. In this instance, agree with the statement in a way that demonstrates both a grasp of your job and the interviewer's statement. For example: 'That's an excellent point, Mr Smith, I couldn't agree more that the attention to detail you describe naturally affects cost containment. My track record in this area...'

Example 7. The interviewer asks a continuing stream of negative questions (as described in Chapter 11).
Response. Use the techniques and answers described earlier. Give your answers with a smile and do not take these questions as personal insults; they are not intended that way. The more stressful the situations the job is likely to place you in, the greater the likelihood of having to field negative questions. The interviewer wants to know if you can take the heat.

Example 8. The interviewer has difficulty looking at you while speaking.
Response. The interviewer is someone who finds it uncomfortable being in the spotlight. Try to help him or her to be a good audience. Ask specific questions about the job responsibilities and offer your skills in turn: 'Would it be of value to you if I described...'

Multiple interviewers

Often an interviewing manager will arrange for you to meet two or three other people. Frequently, these other interviewers have neither been trained in the appropriate interviewing skills nor told the details of the job for which you are interviewing. So you will take additional copies of your executive briefing with you to the interview to aid these additional interviewers in focusing on the appropriate job functions.

When you understand how to recognise and respond to these different types of interviewer, you will leave your interview having made a favourable first impression. No one forgets first impressions.

Chapter 14
The Graceful Exit

To paraphrase Shakespeare, all the world's a stage and all the people on it merely players making their entrances and exits. Curtains rise and fall, and your powerful performance must be capped with a professional and memorable exit. To ensure you leave the right impression, this chapter will review the do's and don'ts of leaving an interview.

A signal that the interview is drawing to a close comes when you are asked whether you have any final questions. Ask your own questions, and by doing so, highlight your strengths and show your enthusiasm. Your goal at the interview is to generate a job offer, so you should find it easy to avoid the crimes that damage your case.

Don'ts

1. Do not discuss salary, vacation, or benefits. It is not that the questions are invalid, just that the timing is wrong. Bringing these topics up before you have an offer is asking what the company can do for you; instead, you should be saying what you can do for the company. These topics are part of the nego-tiation, and without an offer you have nothing to negotiate.

2. Don't press for an early decision. Interviewees *should* ask: 'When will I know your decision?' On hearing the answer, how-ever, they should *not* ask for a decision to be made earlier. And *don't* try to use 'the-other-opportunities-I-have-to-consider' gambit as leverage. This annoys the interviewer, makes you look foolish, and makes you negotiate from a position of weakness. Timing is everything, and how to handle 'other opportunities' as leverage, *correctly*, is handled later in Part 4.

3. Don't show discouragement. Sometimes a job offer can occur on the spot. Most times it does not. Don't show discouragement if you are not offered the job at the interview, because it shows a lack of self-esteem and determination. Avoiding a bad impression is merely the foundation of leaving a good one. The right image to leave is one of enthusiasm, guts, and openness — just the traits you have been projecting throughout the interview.

4. Don't ask for an evaluation of your interview performance. That forces the issue and puts the interviewer in an awkward position.

Do's

1. When the opportunity comes to ask any final questions, review your notes. Bring up any relevant strengths that haven't been addressed. Ask job-related questions.

2. Show decisiveness. If you are offered the job, accept it with enthusiasm. Lock it up now and put yourself in control; you can always change your mind later.

3. When you are interviewed by more than one person, be sure you have the correct spelling of their names. 'I enjoyed meeting your colleagues, Ms Smith. Could you give me the correct spelling of their names please?' This question will give you the names you forgot in the heat of battle, and will demonstrate your consideration.

4. Review the job's requirements with the interviewer and match them point by point with your skills and attributes.

5. Find out if this is the only interview. If so, you must ask for the job in a positive and enthusiastic manner. Find out the time-scale for a decision and finish with: 'I am very enthusiastic about the job and the contributions I can make. If your decision will be made by the 15th, what must I do in the meantime to assure I get the job?'

6. Ask for the next interview. When there are subsequent interviews in the hiring procedure, ask for the next interview in the same honest and forthright manner. 'Is now a good time to arrange our next meeting?' If you do not ask, you do not get.

7. A good leading question to ask is, 'Until I hear from you again, what particular aspects of the job and this interview should I be considering?'

8. Always depart in the same polite and assured manner with which you entered. Look the interviewer in the eyes, put a smile in your baby blue eyes (there's no need to grin), give a firm handshake, and say, 'This has been an exciting meeting for me. This is a job I can do, and I feel I can contribute to your goals, because the atmosphere here seems conducive to doing my very best work. When do we speak again?'

Part 4
Finishing Touches

The successful completion of the first meeting is a big stride towards getting job offers, yet it is not the end of your job hunt.

A company rarely hires the first competent person it sees. In the climate of the 80s, a company has a vast field from which to choose. A manager will sometimes interview as many as 15 people for a particular job, but the strain and pace of conducting interviews naturally dim the memory of each applicant. Unless you are the last person to be interviewed, the impression you make will fade with each subsequent interview the interviewer undertakes. And if you are not remembered, you will not be offered the job. You must develop a strategy to keep your name and skills constantly in the forefront of the interviewer's mind. These finishing touches often make all the difference.

Some of the suggestions here may not seem earth-shattering, but merely a demonstration of your manners, enthusiasm, and determination. But remember that today *all* employers are looking for people with that extra little *something*, so you must avoid the negative (or indifferent) impression that is created when you ignore these guidelines.

Chapter 15
Out of Sight, Out of Mind

The first thing you do on leaving the interview is breathe a sigh
of relief. The second is to make sure that 'out of sight, out of
mind' will not apply to you. You do this by starting a follow-up
procedure immediately after the interview.

Sitting in your car, on the bus or train, do a written recap of
the interview while it's still fresh in your mind. Answer these
questions:

- Who did you meet? Names and titles.
- What does the job entail?
- Why can you do the job?
- What aspects of the interview went poorly? Why?
- What is the agreed next step?
- What was said during the last few minutes of the interview?

Probably the most difficult — and most important — thing to do
is to analyse what aspects of the interview went poorly. A person
does not get offered a job based solely on strength. On the
contrary, many people get new jobs based on their relative lack
of negatives as compared to the other applicants. So, it is
mandatory that you look for and recognise any negatives from
your performance. This is the only way you will have an opportunity to package and overcome those negatives in your follow-up
procedure and during subsequent interviews.

The next step is to write the follow-up letter to the interviewer
to acknowledge the meeting, and keep you fresh in his or her
mind.

1. Type the letter. It exhibits greater professionalism. If you
don't own a typewriter, a typing service will do it for a nominal
fee. If, for any reason, the letter cannot be typed, make sure it
is legibly and neatly written. The letter should make three points
clear to the company representative:

- You paid attention to what was being said.
- You understood the importance of the interviewer's

comments.

- You are excited about the job, can do it, and want it.

2. Use the right words and phrases in your letter. Here are some you might want to use:

- *Upon reflection,* and, *Having thought about our meeting...*
- *Recognise* — 'I recognise the importance of...'
- *Listen* — 'Listening to the points you made...'
- *Enthusiasm, enthusiastic* — Let the interviewer catch your enthusiasm. It is very effective, especially as your letter will arrive while other applicants are nervously sweating their way through the interview.
- *Impressed* — Let the interviewer know you were impressed with the people/product/service/facility/market/position, but *do not overkill.*
- *Challenge* — Feel you would be challenged to do your best work in this environment.
- *Confidence* — There is a job to be done and a challenge to be met. Let the interviewer know you are confident of doing both well.
- *Interest* — If you want the job/next interview, say so. At this stage, the company is buying and you are selling. Ask for the job in a positive and enthusiastic manner.
- *Appreciation* — As a courtesy and mark of professional manners, you must express appreciation for the time the interviewer took out of his or her busy timetable.

3. Whenever possible and appropriate, mention the names of the people you met at the interview. Draw attention to one of the topics that was of general interest to the interviewer(s).

4. Your follow-up letter will be addressed to the main interviewer. Send a copy to personnel with a note of thanks as a courtesy.

5. Send the letter within 24 hours of the interview. If the decision is going to be made in the next couple of days, hand-deliver the letter. The follow-up letter will help to set you apart from other applicants and will refresh your image in the mind of the interviewer just when it would normally be starting to dim.

6. If you do not hear anything after five days, which is quite normal, put in a telephone call to the company representative. Reiterate the points made in the letter, saying that you want the job/next interview, and finish your statements with a question: 'Mr Smith, I feel confident about my ability to contribute to your department's efforts and I really want the job. Could you tell me what I have to do to get it?' Then be quiet and wait for the answer.

Of course, you may be told that you are no longer in the running. The next chapter will show you that this is a *great* opportunity to snatch victory from the jaws of defeat.

Chapter 16

Snatching Victory from the Jaws of Defeat

During the interviewing process, there are bound to be interviewers who *erroneously* come to the conclusion that you are not the right person for the job they need to fill. When this happens, you will be turned down. This absurd travesty of justice can occur in different ways:

- At the interview
- In a letter of rejection
- During your follow-up telephone call.

Whenever the turn-down comes, you must be emotionally and intellectually prepared to take advantage of the *opportunity* being offered to you.

When you get turned down for the only opportunity you have going, the rejection can be devastating to your ego. That is why I have stressed throughout the wisdom of having at least a few interviews in train at the same time. This naturally does not apply if you are fortunate enough to be represented by a skilled personnel consultant. He or she will naturally have lined up the best opportunities for you to begin with.

You *will* get turned down. No one can be right for every job. However, the right person for a job doesn't always get it; the best prepared and most determined often does. While you may be responsible in part for the initial rejection, you still have the power to correct the situation and win the job offer. What you do with the claimed victory is a different matter; you will then be in a seller's market with choice and control of your situation.

To correct this requires only willpower and determination. Almost every job you desire is obtainable once you understand the process from the interviewer's side of the desk. Your initial — and temporary — rejection is attributable to only one of these reasons:

- Interviewer does not feel you can do the job.
- Interviewer feels you lack a successful profile.

- Interviewer did not feel your personality would contribute to the smooth functioning of the department.

With belief in yourself, you can still succeed. Repeat to yourself constantly through the interview cycle: 'I will get this job, no one else can give as much to this company as I can!' Do this and implement the following plan immediately when you hear of rejection, whether in person, by letter, or over the telephone.

Step 1. Thank the interviewer for the time and consideration. Then ask politely: 'To help my future job search, why wasn't I chosen for the position?' Assure the interviewer that you would truly appreciate honest and objective reasoning. Listen to the reply and do not interrupt regardless of the comments. Use your time constructively and take notes furiously. When the company representative finishes speaking, show you understood the comments. (Remember, understanding and agreeing are different animals.)

'Thank you, Mr Smith, now I can understand the way you feel. Because I am not a professional interviewer, I'm afraid my interview nerves got in the way. I'm very interested in working for your company *(use an enthusiastic tone)*, and am determined to get the job. Let me meet you once again. This time, when I'm not so nervous, I am confident you will see I really do have the skills/attributes you require *(then provide an example of a skill you have in the questionable area)*. You name the time and the place, and I will be there. What's best for you, Mr Smith?'

End with a question, of course. An enthusiastic request like this is very difficult to refuse and will usually get you another interview. An interview, of course, at which you *must* shine.

Step 2. Check your notes and accept the company representative's concerns. Their validity is irrelevant; the important point is that these negative points represent the problem areas in the interviewer's perception of you. List the negative perceptions, and using the techniques, exercises, and value keys discussed throughout the book, develop different ways to overcome or compensate for every negative perception.

Step 3. Re-read Part 3.

Step 4. Practise aloud the statements and responses you will use at the interview. If you can practise with someone who plays the part of the interviewer, so much the better. This will create a real interview atmosphere and be helpful to your success.

Step 5. Study *all* available information on the company.

Step 6. Congratulate yourself continually for getting another interview after initial rejection. This is proof of your self-worth, ability, and tenacity. You have nothing to lose and everything to gain, having already risen phoenix-like from the ashes of temporary defeat.

Step 7. During the interview, ask for the job in a positive and enthusiastic manner. Your drive and staying power will impress the interviewer. All you must do to win the job is overcome the perceived negatives, and you have been given the time to prepare. Go for it.

Step 8. Even when all has failed at the subsequent interview, do not leave without a final request for the job. Play your trump card: 'Mr Smith, I respect the fact that you allowed me the opportunity to prove myself here today. I am convinced I am the best person for the job. I want you to give me a trial and I will prove on the job that I am the best appointment you have made this year. Will you give us both the opportunity?'

Most people fail in their endeavours by quitting just before the dawn of success. Follow these directions and you can win the job. You have proved yourself to be a fighter and that is universally admired. The company representative will want you to succeed because you are made of stuff that is rarely seen today. You are a person of guts, drive, and endurance, the hallmarks of a winner. Job turn-downs are an opportunity to exercise and build your strengths, and you may well add to your growing number of job offers.

Chapter 17

Multiple Interviews, Multiple Offers

False optimism and laziness lead many job hunters to be content with only one interview in view at any given time. This severely reduces the odds of landing the best job in town within your chosen time-scale. It further guarantees that you will continue to operate in a buyer's market.

The recommended approach is to generate as many interviews as possible in a two- to three-week period. Interviewing skills are learned, and necessarily improve with practice. With the improved skills comes a greater confidence, and those natural interview nerves disperse. Your confidence shows through to potential employers, and you are perceived in a positive light. And because other companies are interested in you, everyone will move more quickly to secure your services. This is especially important if you are unfortunate enough to be unemployed. Being out of work is when you need money the most and is the time when the salary you can command on the open market is substantially reduced. The interview activity you generate will help offset this.

By generating multiple interviews, you bring the time of the first job offer closer and closer. That one job offer can be quickly exploited to produce a number of others. And with a single job offer, your unemployed status has, to all intents and purposes, passed.

Immediately you can ring every company that interviewed you and explain the situation. 'Mr Johnson, I'm phoning because, while still under consideration by your company, I have received a job offer from one of your competitors. I would hate to make a decision without the chance of speaking to you again. I was very impressed by my meeting with you. Can we get together in the next couple of days?' End, of course, with a question that carries the conversation forward.

If you were in the running at all, your call will usually generate another interview or speed the decision; Mr Johnson does not want to miss out on a suddenly prized commodity. Remember:

it is human nature to want the very things one is about to lose. So you see, your simple offer can be multiplied almost by the number of interviews you have in process at the time.

A single job offer can also be used to generate interviews with new firms. It is as simple as making your usual telephone networking presentation, but ending it differently. You would be very interested in meeting them because of (your knowledge of the company/product/service), but also because you have just received a job offer. Would it be possible to get together in the next couple of days?

Relying on one interview at a time can only lead to prolonged anxiety, disappointment, and possibly unemployment. This reliance is due to the combination of false optimism, laziness, and fear of rejection. These are traits that cannot be tolerated except by confirmed defeatists, for defeat is the inevitable result of these traits. As Heraclitus said, 'Character is destiny.' In the employment business we say, 'The job offer that cannot fail will.'

Self-esteem, on the other hand, is vital to your success, and happiness is found with it. And with it you will awake each day with a vitality previously unknown. Vigour will increase, your enthusiasm will rise, and desire to achieve will burn within. The more you do today, the better you will feel tomorrow.

Even when you follow this plan to the letter, not every interview will result in an offer. But with many irons in the fire, an occasional firm rejection should not affect your morale. If it does, grow up! This won't be the first or last time you face rejection. Be persistent, and above all, close your mind to all negative and discouraging influences. The success you experience from implementing this plan will increase your store of willpower and determination, penetrate to the core of your being, effect the successful outcome of your job hunt, and enrich your whole life. Start today. The key to your success is preparation. Remember, it is necessary to plan and organise in order to get rich. Staying poor is easy; poverty needs no effort. Tomorrow never comes, so start building that well-stocked briefcase today.

Conclusion: The Glittering Prizes

It's time for action, to wrestle job offers from the other contenders at the job interview. All victories have their foundation in careful preparation, and in finishing this book, you are equipped and ready for the hunt.

Your winning attitude is positive and active (dream jobs don't come to those who sit and wait), you realise success depends on getting out and generating interviews for yourself. At these interviews you will maintain the interviewer's interest and attention by carrying your half of the conversation. What you ask will show your interest, demonstrate your analytical abilities, and carry the conversation forward. If in doubt about the meaning of a question, you will ask one of your own to clarify it.

The corporate body recognises its most valuable resources in those employees who understand and contribute towards its goals. These people have something in common: they all recognise their differing jobs as a series of challenges and problems; each to be anticipated, met, and solved. It's this attitude that lands jobs and helps careers.

People like this advance their careers faster than others, because they possess a critical awareness of universally admired business practices and value systems. They then gear up their careers by projecting the personality traits that most closely complement those practices and values.

As I said at the beginning of this book, a job interview is a ritualised mating dance. The name of that dance is 'attitude'. Now that you know the steps, you are ready to whirl away with the glittering prizes. There is no more to say except: go to your next interview and *knock 'em for six.*

Bibliography

Some of the books listed here can be bought inexpensively in a bookshop. Most, however, are expensive, so you will find it cost-effective to go to your local library to use them. Many boroughs have an inter-library lending system, so if the book you want is not available, the librarian can usually get it for you.

As mentioned earlier, do not rely *solely* on reference books. Their size and scope often make them a little out of date, and they aren't all updated or published every year. Ask your librarian for the most recent editions.

Business directories and company information

Britain's Top Private Companies, Jordan & Sons Ltd, Jordan House, 47 Brunswick Place, London N1 6EE.

Extel Statistical Services, Extel, 37-45 Paul Street, London EC2A 4PB.

Jordan's Business Reports, Jordan's Business Information Service, Jordan House, 47 Brunswick Place, London N1 6EE.

Kelly's Manufacturers and Merchants Directory, annual, Business Press International Ltd, Quadrant House, The Quadrant, Sutton, Surrey SM2 5AS.

Key British Enterprises, Dun & Bradstreet, 26-32 Clifton Street, London EC2P 2LY.

Kompass, Kompass Publishers Ltd, Windsor Court, East Grinstead House, East Grinstead, West Sussex RH19 1XD.

Principal International Businesses, Dun & Bradstreet; address above.

Sell's Directory, annual, Sell's Publications Ltd., 55 High Street, Epsom, Surrey KT19 8DW.

The Stock Exchange Official Yearbook, annual, Macmillan Publishers Ltd, Houndmills, Basingstoke, Hampshire.

The Times 1000, 1985-86, Times Books, 16 Golden Square, London W1R 4BN.

Who Owns Whom, Dun & Bradstreet; address above.

The World Directory of Multinational Enterprises, 1980, Macmillan; address above.

Employment

British Qualifications, annual, Kogan Page, 120 Pentonville Road, London N1 9JN.

Changing Your Job After 35, 5th edn, 1984, Godfrey Golzen and Philip Plumbley, Kogan Page; address above.

Directory of Opportunities in New Technology, annual, Kogan Page; address above.

Employment Gazette, Department of Employment; on subscription, monthly. HMSO.

Executive Post, Manpower Services Commission, Professional and Executive Recruitment, 2-4 Fitzwilliam Gate, Sheffield S1 4JH. Free.

Getting There: Jobhunting for Women, 1987 (in preparation), Margaret Wallis, Kogan Page; address above.

Technical Employment: A Handbook for Professional Engineers and Technologists, and Recruiters, annual, Michael Still, Kogan Page; address above.

Working Abroad: The Daily Telegraph Guide, 9th edn, 1986, Godfrey Golzen, Kogan Page; address above.

The Kogan Page Careers Series

This series consists of short guides (96-168 pages) to different careers for school-leavers, graduates and anyone wanting to start anew. Each book serves as an introduction to a particular career and to jobs available within that field, including full details of training qualifications and courses. The following 'Careers in' titles are available in paperback; each measures 180 x 110 mm.

Accountancy (*2nd edition in preparation*)
Agriculture and Agricultural Sciences
Alternative Medicine
Antiques
Architecture
The Army
Art and Design (*3rd edition*)
Aviation
Banking
Business
Catering and Hotel Management (*2nd edition*)
The Church
Civil Engineering
Civil Service
Classical Music
Computers and Information Technology (*4th edition in preparation*)
Conservation (*2nd edition*)
Crafts
Dance

Electrical and Electronic Engineering (*2nd edition in preparation*)
Engineering
Eye Care
Fashion
Film Industry
Floristry and Retail Gardening
Hairdressing and Beauty Therapy (*3rd edition*)
Holiday Industry
Home Economics
Insurance
Journalism (*2nd edition*)
Land and Property
The Law (*2nd edition*)
Librarianship and Information Science
Local Government
Marketing, Public Relations and Advertising (*3rd edition in preparation*)
Medicine, Dentistry and Mental Health (*2nd edition*)

Modelling
Museums and Art Galleries
Music Business
Nursing and Allied Professions
  (*3rd edition*)
Oil and Gas
Pharmacy
Photography
The Police Force
Politics
Printing
Psychology
Publishing
Retailing (*2nd edition*)
Road Transport
At Sea
Secretarial and Office Work
  (*3rd edition*)

Social Work (*2nd edition*)
Sport
Surveying
Teaching
Telecommunications
Television and Radio (*2nd edition*)
The Theatre (*2nd edition in preparation*)
Using Biology
Using Languages (*2nd edition*)
Using Mathematics
Veterinary Surgery
Working Abroad
Working Outdoors (*2nd edition*)
Working with Animals (*3rd edition*)
Working with Children
Working with the Disabled
Working with Horses